POETS IN BRIEF

ALFRED, LORD TENNYSON

ALFRED, LORD TENNYSON
An Anthology

Chosen by
F. L. LUCAS
*Fellow of King's College
Cambridge*

Ἀλλὰ φίλοις μὲν ἐμοῖσι φέρω χάριν, ἔστι δὲ μύσταις
κοινὸς ὁ τῶν Μουσέων ἡδυεπὴς στέφανος.

MELEAGER

CAMBRIDGE
AT THE UNIVERSITY PRESS
1932

PROPERTY OF
HIGH POINT PUBLIC LIBRARY
HIGH POINT, NORTH CAROLINA

CAMBRIDGE
UNIVERSITY PRESS

University Printing House, Cambridge CB2 8BS, United Kingdom

Published in the United States of America by Cambridge University Press, New York

Cambridge University Press is part of the University of Cambridge.

It furthers the University's mission by disseminating knowledge in the pursuit of education, learning and research at the highest international levels of excellence.

www.cambridge.org
Information on this title: www.cambridge.org/9781107682832

© Cambridge University Press 1932

This publication is in copyright. Subject to statutory exception and to the provisions of relevant collective licensing agreements, no reproduction of any part may take place without the written permission of Cambridge University Press.

First published 1932
First paperback edition 2014

A catalogue record for this publication is available from the British Library

ISBN 978-1-107-68283-2 Paperback

Cambridge University Press has no responsibility for the persistence or accuracy of URLs for external or third-party internet websites referred to in this publication, and does not guarantee that any content on such websites is, or will remain, accurate or appropriate.

To

ANNE BARNES

CONTENTS

PREFATORY NOTE	PAGE xi
INTRODUCTION	xiii
The Devil and the Lady	1
Claribel	7
Supposed Confessions of a Second-rate Sensitive Mind	8
Mariana	10
To ——	13
Ode to Memory	13
Song	14
A Character	15
The Dying Swan	16
A Dirge	17
Lisette	19
Milton's Mulberry	21
The Lady of Shalott	22
The Two Voices	28
The Miller's Daughter	30
Fatima	31
Œnone	32
The Palace of Art	41
The May Queen	52
The Lotos-Eaters	52
A Dream of Fair Women	58
To J. S.	69
On a Mourner	72

'Love Thou thy Land'	73
The Lover's Tale	73
Sonnet	74
Morte d'Arthur	74
The Gardener's Daughter	83
Love and Duty	85
Ulysses	86
Tithonus	88
Godiva	91
Sir Launcelot and Queen Guinevere	91
A Farewell	93
The Eagle	93
'Come not, when I am dead'	94
The Vision of Sin	94
To E. L., on his Travels in Greece	102
'Break, break, break...'	103
The Princess, A Medley	104
In Memoriam A. H. H.	108
Maud, A Monodrama	128
The Daisy	133
To the Rev. F. D. Maurice	137
In the Valley of Cauteretz	138
In the Garden at Swainston	139
Requiescat	139
'Flower in the crannied wall'	140
Specimen of a Translation of the Iliad in Blank Verse	140
Enoch Arden	140

Aylmer's Field	142
Lucretius	143
Idylls of the King:	
The Coming of Arthur	
The Tale of Bleys	152
Gareth and Lynette	
Gareth's First Adventure	154
Geraint and Enid	
The Meeting of Geraint and Enid	154
Geraint scatters the followers of Limours	155
Their Reconciliation	156
Merlin and Vivien	
Merlin's Foreboding	156
The Dawn of Arthur's Reign	157
Vivien's Song	158
The Emptiness of Fame	159
The Tale of Merlin's Spell	159
Merlin's Fall	163
Lancelot and Elaine	
The Finding of the Diamonds of the Tournament	164
Guinevere on Arthur	164
Sir Lancelot's Kindred ride him down	165
The End of Elaine	166
Sir Lancelot's Remorse	168
The Holy Grail	
Arthur's Hall	170
Arthur's City	171

The Holy Grail (contd.)
    The Passing of Sir Galahad 172
    Sir Lancelot's Quest for the Grail . . . 174

Pelleas and Ettarre
    Song before Guinevere 176
    The Return of Sir Pelleas 176

The Last Tournament
    King Arthur and the Red Knight . . . 177
    The Burning of the Red Knight's Tower . . 177

Guinevere
    Guinevere's Flight 178
    Modred Remembers 178
    The Signs at Arthur's Coming 178
    The Parting of Arthur and Guinevere . . 181

The Passing of Arthur
    The End of Arthur's Last Battle . . . 182

The Revenge 182
The Voyage of Maeldune 188
Tiresias 196
Locksley Hall Sixty Years After 196
To Virgil 197
'Frater Ave atque Vale' 199
The Progress of Spring 199
Merlin and the Gleam 204
June Bracken and Heather 208
St Telemachus 209
Crossing the Bar 209

PREFATORY NOTE

I HAVE to thank Mr C. B. L. Tennyson for his very generous leave to reprint here the poems *Lisette*, *Milton's Mulberry* (for which I offer my apologies to Christ's College, Cambridge), and 'How thought you that this thing could captivate?' from his series of articles on his grandfather's unpublished work in the *Nineteenth Century* for March–June, 1931; and also for permission to take extracts from that fascinating work, *The Devil and the Lady*, first published in 1930. The copyright poems are reprinted by arrangement with Messrs Macmillan & Co., Ltd.

F. L. L.

King's College
Cambridge
December 1931

INTRODUCTION

ANTHOLOGIES have recently been attacked by critics of a certain kind. But anthologies continue to be read. Men have always cried that life is short; it has never seemed shorter than to-day when the world lives faster than ever before. Certainly life is not long enough for mediocre poetry; and few poets have escaped writing a good deal of that. Tennyson was no exception; while now that just over a century lies between us and his first appearance in our literature he is remote enough for at all events some agreement, not indeed how good he is, but what is best in him. That I have tried to embody here; together with certain other things of his which have perhaps not had their due of recognition.

There is, however, a further feature in this book which may outrage not only those who regard anthologies as works of the Evil One, but others less petulant. It contains not only whole poems, but fragments of poems. What a strange charm fragments can have I first found from those that survive, often tantalizing in their brevity, from lost Greek tragedy. There is indeed a great deal of truth in the observation of Proust: 'Justement en citant ainsi un vers isolé, on décuple sa puissance attractive'. These isolated passages will, as I say, probably irritate some readers; just as, by the common lot of anthologies, the omission of their favourite pieces will irritate others; but I hope the general result may be to leave a further number less blindly irritated against Tennyson himself. For, taken as a whole, he exasperates the present generation so badly that they have not patience to find out what is best in him, or to value it when they find it, embedded as it is in so much that they hate or ridicule. The young to-day tend to feel towards him as the rebellious Amoret towards her old Magician in the first extract in this book—

> Go thy ways!
> Thou yellowest leaf on Autumn's wither'd tree!
> Thou sickliest ear of all the sheaf!

But the old Magician has not lost his magic for all that.

The truth is, I think, that Tennyson is still too close to us, even now, to be seen with a real sense of proportion. He was supremely typical of his age—its Poet Laureate, its chosen and accepted singer, as no other English poet in his own lifetime has ever been; and there are few literary laws so invariable as that what is meat and drink to one age is poison or dishwater to the next. The particular qualities which the writers of an era bring to perfection, since they cannot be surpassed, are very naturally disparaged by their successors; while their faults and follies, even their foibles, even their virtues made tedious at last by satiety, seem less forgivable than any others in the world. This quite normal literary reaction of the twentieth century against the nineteenth, answering to that of the nineteenth against the classicism of the eighteenth, has, however, been intensified by a moral and social reaction of a violence unparalleled in England since Charles II landed at Dover. We view the age of Tennyson as the Restoration viewed the age of Cromwell. The cause in either case is exactly the same. No sin on earth brings upon itself in the end such a retribution of rage and derision as over-righteousness. No reign in our history before Victoria's, not even the riotous incompetence of the Restoration, has goaded the succeeding age to such savage satire as the Reign of the Saints provoked in *Hudibras.* Other generations have been suffered by their children to sleep peacefully in their dust; but on the graves of Obadiah-bind-their-kings-in-chains and Zeal-of-the-land-busy, of Pecksniff and Chadband, posterity has clapped its hands and danced.

But even if one may read running, it is not easy to judge dancing. When the present age finds fault with Tennyson, we cannot take it for granted that the fault is always Tennyson's. The case against him is indeed simple—much too simple. He seems to-day, as Matthew Arnold said long since, 'deficient in intellectual power'; or as a modern critic complains, 'In the only province about which a poet should cherish a deep concern, he had made no progress whatever. He was no nearer reality than before'.

Now a great philosophic poet Tennyson was not. His contemporaries at Cambridge expected and encouraged him to become one; many of his contemporaries in later years thought he had actually succeeded; but to us his view of the world seems a palsied compromise, shaking its head helplessly between science and faith, between the optimism of his age and his own inborn melancholy, between his fear of life and an even deeper dread of death, that insisted with impotent desperation on personal immortality.

But since when, we may well ask, has it been established that good poets must be also good philosophers? Plato banished the poets from his Utopia precisely because he found their philosophy always so bad. A poet must indeed have opinions about existence; everyone must, who is not half-witted; and a creative writer in particular needs some fairly coherent view of life to provide a coherent background to his work. But that is mainly an aesthetic need; it is coherence that matters rather than truth. For, after all, the writers of the world have held a hundred contradictory creeds; even could we know which was right, should we then burn the rest?

To decry poets on the ground that they are not profound thinkers is to curse the vine of Dionysus for not bearing Apples of Knowledge. Certainly few poets could pass such a Test Act. If Tennyson fails, was Spenser then so clear-headed, with the muddled Platonism and copy-book morals of the *Faerie Queene*? Or Milton, with the grotesque theological machinery of *Paradise Lost*, as shocking by modern standards of justice and good sense as anything that Xenophanes denounced in Homer and Hesiod? Or Dryden, with the schoolboy logic of *Religio Laici* and *The Hind and the Panther*? Or Pope, with the borrowed philosophy of the *Essay on Man*, so little worth the borrowing? Or Wordsworth, groping and stumbling in a mountain-mist of lofty sentiments between God and Nature, Pantheism and the Established Church? It is seldom that a gift for logic and a gift for imaginative creation go together; as well demand that poets should excel in physics, as in metaphysics. Even distinguished scientists, as we have recently had opportunities of noting, are apt to stagger terribly when they trespass across the frontiers of philosophy; while on the other hand even philosophers, such is the power of purely poetic qualities in and by themselves, may sometimes continue, like Plato, to move readers who find their reasoning fantastic, by gifts of imagination and style alone. The type of critic who is always judging poets by their ideas might pause to consider two remarks of one of the most thoughtful of all poets, Goethe—'I have always kept myself free from philosophy'; and again—'They come and ask me "What idea I meant to embody in my *Faust*?" as if I knew myself and could tell them'. Nightingales are not made for cracking nuts. No doubt when a poet does express our own personal attitude to the Universe, there is an even deeper pleasure of sympathy in reading him; for those who share Hardy's view of things, few writers in all literature can be as poignant as he; but such pleasure is an enhancement, not an essential. Sensible readers learn not to hope for much reasoning power from poets; and for the sake of their enjoyment find little difficulty in suspending their disbelief. Lucretius and Dante cannot both be right about the future of the soul; neither may be; but that is secondary. A writer of genius creates a world of his own; we are under no compulsion to travel there; but if we do, we must not expect its laws and constitution to be necessarily the same as those the real world seems to us to show. To ask more is to embrace that dead idea, reborn at the Renaissance but moribund more than a century ago, that poetry must 'teach'. With older writers, whose battlefields of controversy time has softened to green mounds where only their poetry still flowers, a forgetful tolerance of their philosophic imbecilities comes easy to us; but with Tennyson we find it harder to agree to differ. The dead Victorians still hang gibbeted before the world's mockery, as the dead Cromwell and Ireton were torn up from the Abbey, where they had been laid so pompously, to rot high on Tyburn; but the future, more indifferent to the cleverness of 1932, will be more merciful—and juster—to the past.

It may indeed be answered that there is more against Tennyson than mere incompetence as a thinker; that there is also insincerity. He was intellectually dishonest, it is said. The generation of to-day is maddened or sickened to find him expounding views of love and morals, of progress and politics, against the cant of which in the mouths of parents or schoolmasters their own youth revolted or is still revolting. Tennyson's metaphysics, they feel, may have been poor but honest, though even there he cheated a good deal in letting the wish be father to the thought; but his moralizing they find past all endurance. The *Idylls of the King* are the apotheosis of a prig; his discussion of feminism begins in a picnic and is drowned by a wedding-bell; his politics consisted at home in hedging, abroad in that type of cackling bluster which was to end in hatching, to its own ridiculous consternation, the dragon's egg of the War. There can be no use and no excuse, they feel, for the writer of lines like—

And that good man, the clergyman, has told me words of peace;

or—

Household happiness, gracious children, debtless competence, golden mean;

no quarter for one who could paint a happy wife in such tones of emetic pink as—

> And all the wisdom that she has
> Is to love him for being wise.

This is indeed a more serious charge. Weakness is more unpoetic, and more damaging to a poet, than wickedness; and weakness of heart than weakness of head. But here too time brings readier tolerance. We forgive and forget the weaknesses and insincerities of older poets, the grovelling flatteries to which Virgil and Spenser, Donne and Dryden did not hesitate to stoop; we see such things more calmly now, as dust of the world they lived in, which soils even the whiteness of the Immortals as they pass across the earth. So too the meannesses of Pope find shrill defence to-day. Tennyson was incapable of such things; but he is nearer to us and to the quick of our prejudices.

The only sane course is to enjoy the good in writers and forget the rest. Tennyson writes badly when he is being a lay-preacher, or Dryden when he is being a lick-spittle; what signifies is that there were other times when they wrote well.

It has indeed become almost hackneyed, since it was first so convincingly stated by Mr Harold Nicholson, and yet it still remains amazing, what a dual personality existed in Tennyson. His work resembles some lofty rock-face with a soft streak in it that has weathered badly. Bred in the bracing east winds of Lincolnshire, the son (in a family of twelve) of a stern and gloomy rector, he inherited from the father's side a physique gipsy-like in its darkness and, latterly, in its unkemptness, but so noble in its massive strength that at first sight Carlyle forgave him the frivolity of being a poet; and, with it, a temperament of mingled bluntness and sadness. But the soft streak, feminine and hysterical, was also there; derived from his mother and deepened by the circumstances of life, which contained indeed a good deal of passive suffering, especially in its earlier half, but was lacking in active experience. This side of him appears already in the mawkishness of early poems like *The Darling Room*, in his relations with Hallam, in his hysteria about being criticized, even at Cambridge; but it was in middle and later life that the weaker Tennyson became more and more vocal, with the tones of a rather acrimonious spinster. The hero of *Locksley Hall* (1842) has already the shrill accents that mark his family likeness to the neurotic heroes of *The Princess* (1847) and *Maud* (1855); with *The Princess* appears also that unfortunate figure, 'the Maiden Aunt'—

> Then the Maiden Aunt
> Took this fair day for text, and from it preached
> An universal culture for the crowd,
> And all things great.

There is a terrible touch of unconscious self-parody in this personage, with her 'preaching', and her 'universal culture for the crowd', and the typical vague sublimity of 'all things great'. More and more, I think, one comes to agree with the affectionate but uncompromising criticisms of Fitzgerald—his despair at *The Princess*, his complaint that even *In Memoriam* three years later, though 'full of the finest things', yet 'has that air of being ground out by a Poetic Machine of the highest order', his obstinate conviction that Tennyson was never really himself again after the volume of 1842. To the very end of his life the old poet remained capable of bursting suddenly into poetry that no familiarity can contemn, down to his final *Nunc Dimittis* of *Crossing the Bar*; but after 1842 his weaker self began to grow too strong for him; he became more and more subdued to the age he worked in, more self-conscious before his audience, more anxious about improving them. This was unfortunate, because he sang best when he was thinking least of making his hearers better. The Lotos-eaters would have shocked the Ancient Sage; but, idle creatures as they are, they have done a good deal better service than that tedious elder to their author's memory. *Tithonus*, perhaps Tennyson's most perfect thing, might surprise us by its apparent date; for it was published only in 1860, and it seems late to be so good; but a letter of the poet's reveals that it too was composed more than a quarter of a century before. It was indeed inevitable that after 1850, as he became more and more the Laureate of the Empire, a sense of moral responsibility should grow upon him, so that from a singer he tended to become a mouthpiece, and to write for his own age instead of for all time; until the magnificent young poet of the bust by Woolner in Trinity College Library had grown gradually more like, if never really like, the dim and moss-grown mystic of the painting by Watts in Trinity College Hall.

It is tempting to ask if Tennyson might not have done greater things, had he been forced in his middle and later years to face, instead of the snug security of Farringford and

Aldworth, a harder destiny in a sterner world, like Dante or Milton. The Lincolnshire vigour in him was fit for something better than the relaxing softness of the Isle of Wight, with nothing more exciting to break its even tenour than a letter from the Queen or a visit from General Garibaldi. There in the glades of Farringford, unseen, the lotus grew. Such an atmosphere of eternal afternoon encouraged the tendency in him to write like Florian, whose pastorals, it was said, had never a wolf in them; to depict a world without either granite or mud. The early sneer of Lockhart about Tennyson's belonging to 'the Milky Way of poetry' had its sting; and as Tennyson's star rose higher, it tended at times to get lost in the misty brilliance of that vague though exalted path.

And yet how difficult it remains to sum up his or any human character in a few neat phrases, was shown only last year (1930). 'Alfred', said Fitzgerald in another of his fond, but relentless criticisms, 'cannot trifle.' It seemed just; one of the things that irritates our more frivolous generation is the rather portentous earnestness of the Laureate's Collected Works, only relieved here and there by a too elephantine humour. But with the publication in 1930 by Mr C. B. L. Tennyson of *The Devil and the Lady*, written (incredible though it seems) at the age of fourteen, with possible revision up to sixteen, it appears that once upon a time Alfred could 'trifle', and most entertainingly. The verbal music we know so well, is indeed already audible; many readers of the late Lord Tennyson's *Memoir* of his father must have been struck by the fragment already quoted there:

> There is a clock in Pandemonium,
> Hard by the burning throne of my Great Grandsire,
> The slow vibrations of whose pendulum,
> With click-clack alternation to and fro,
> Sound 'EVER, NEVER!' thro' the courts of Hell.

But that gave no idea of the piece as a whole; for this comedy of an old magician's employment of the Devil to guard his young wife Amoret from a ludicrous pack of lovers of every profession, shows a combination of high-spirited character-drawing, wit, and gaiety, that seems the work of a different being in a different world. Not the least surprising thing about this boyish product of a country rectory is the gay freedom of its treatment, curiously cynical at times, of the character of women and of a subject free in itself. That a poet so prudish in his later years, at least on paper, should have written this at fourteen, and that his father, 'the stern Doctor', should have admired and preserved it, may bring home to us some of the outspokenness of that earlier England of George IV and Lord Byron in which the Laureate of Queen Victoria was born and bred. We should find it far easier to love him now if this light-hearted laughter had not died so young in him; but even his share in *Poems by Two Brothers*, written only two or three years later, is dull and solemn; and it is melancholy to contrast this piece of boyish brilliance with the worthy and weary dramas he was to hammer out half a century later.

So hard is it to analyse anything as living and changing as a human being. Still the essential excellences of Tennyson need no discovery. The difficulty remains rather to see with a vision undazed by custom what has long become so familiar. For he has paid the penalty of his own success and suffered the fate that Horace feared, of becoming a classic, dog-eared in the hands and in the weary memories of schoolboys. What will endure in Tennyson is, I believe, above all his Virgilian beauty of language and beauty of landscape, his Virgilian sadness over a world whose sorrows are so painfully plain, whose hopes so dim with mystery.

> The woods decay, the woods decay and fall,
> The vapours weep their burthen to the ground,
> Man comes and tills the field and lies beneath,
> And after many a summer dies the swan.

With these, less often recognized, there goes that vein of Horatian urbanity in poems like *The Daisy* and the lines to F. D. Maurice. But, as has been said, his merits like his faults are harder for us to value than they will be for our children. The human temperament swings like a pendulum between the ideal and the realistic, between the love of Beauty and the love of Truth, between a taste for sugar and a taste for pepper. The noble in literature is out of fashion now. We despise it in Tennyson, as Donne despised it in Spenser. A cult for cynical 'sincerity' has become our peculiar form of cant. Where the literature of the Victorian had too much of the dowager, ours leans to the guttersnipe. We are brighter, more amusing, clever enough to see through everything that is at all transparent, except our own cleverness, and through some things that are not; but our writing is disfigured by its lack of sense and taste, by its fondness for the fantastic and the ignoble. And so, where cleverness tells, there our age succeeds, up to a point; in fiction, in biography, in journalism. But for writing poetry, or judging it, cleverness is curiously inadequate. It is seduced by the tinkling tinsel of the ingenious; it undervalues dignity and restraint. Hence the style of Tennyson is at present sadly out of favour. No doubt his verse is sometimes polished to excess, like the prose of Stevenson; and what Burke says of languages, that the most polished lack strength, is true also of styles. There is an autumnal Alexandrianism about much of Tennyson; an enemy might say that his Muse enamelled her face and the enamel had cracked with time. But time, I believe, will have little power over the sculptured stateliness of his best lyrics and of his shorter pieces of blank verse.

As with beauty of style, so with beauty of landscape; that too, since the Georgian poets, is out of fashion. But this change too is merely fashion. 'To make the much-loved earth', in Sidney's phrase, 'more lovely', will always be a main part of the poet's mission on it. It is a poem like *The Dying Swan* that reveals the true Tennyson—perfect in the painting of its desolation of grey sky and sodden fenland and reeds shivering in the wind; perfect also in the music of its brooding melancholy before the face of death. Tennyson's dignity of sadness may seem milk and water to a generation that either smiles ironically, or slings mud, at life. His sorrowful moonlight may pale before our fireworks; we may think it mere moonshine; but it will return, when the squibs that outshone it have long ceased to bang and stink. Tennyson too might have uttered those words of Matthew Arnold to the monks of the Grande Chartreuse, which anticipate so much that the twentieth century has said against the nineteenth—

> For the world cries your faith is now
> But a dead time's exploded dream;
> My melancholy, sciolists say,
> Is a pass'd mode, an outworn theme—
> As if the world had ever had
> A faith, or sciolists been sad!

But it was not a small thing to have added so much to the household associations of a nation. The Elaines and Enids of to-day may ignore or despise him: willy-nilly, their own names remain living memorials of his power. Mariana and the Lady of Shalott, Arthur and Excalibur, Œnone and the Lotos-eaters have become so much part of our earliest recollections, that we take them for granted and belittle what a feat it was thus to mould and stamp the English mind. What, after all, did the Arthurian legends mean to the ordinary reader before *The Lady of Shalott* in 1832 (derived, curiously enough, from an Italian novel) and the *Morte d'Arthur* in 1842? Things of his like these have become so trite, and are so typical, that they tend to make us undervalue his versatility. But those who imagine that Tennyson wrote, at best, in a limited vein of monotonous perfection, may turn in the pages that follow to pieces like *The Devil and the Lady, Lisette, Milton's Mulberry, Fatima*, the sonnet 'How thought you that this thing could captivate?', *Sir Launcelot and Queen Guinevere*, 'Come not, when I am dead', *The Daisy, Requiescat*, and *The Vision of Sin*; while of his more typical work I hope the fragments from the *Idylls of the King* may show how vivid even those could be, at their best, though failures as a whole. For the years to come Tennyson, I believe, can safely follow the words of Bacon's last testament and bequeath his name and memory 'to mine own country, after some time has passed over'.

Meanwhile, though each year of our progress, as it buries deeper the beliefs he lived by, disfeatures also the very landscapes that bred him what he was, it is still possible to escape from the tar that floods, the yellow brick that entombs, so much of Tennyson's England and find up quiet lanes and over lonely hill-tops the country that was the background and the seed-ground of his purest poetry. For the work of Tennyson recalls above all, I feel, some English parkland like his own Farringford with its sloping lawns and ancient elms, guarded by the great rampart of the downs, as it was before Freshwater too was spoiled. It is something tamer and less rugged than Wordsworth's fells of Westmorland. It is not wild, nor bracing, nor titanic, nor sublime—only a quietly ordered beauty of primrose and daffodil, clanging rookery and crooning dove. Yet it has too a majesty of its own, where its great cliffs drop sheer amid a wail of sea-birds to that sea he sang so well. These indeed are no ill symbols of the beauty of Tennyson—the white cliffs of Freshwater, the sweep of the Sussex downs by Aldworth, the wide skies of Lincolnshire with Lincoln Minster hanging in their distant clouds; just as you may find Hardy in the gaunter, bleaker wastes of sand and pine that make Egdon Heath; or Housman in the lonely forest-pillar of the Wrekin, looking across the stream of Severn, past the ruins of Roman Uricon and Norman Buildwas, to the blue uplands of the West.

THE DEVIL & THE LADY

ACT I, SC. IV

[*The elderly wizard*, Magus, *has just departed on a journey after taking leave of his young wife* Amoret.]

* * *

AMORET.   Go thy ways!
Thou yellowest leaf on Autumn's wither'd tree!
Thou sickliest ear of all the sheaf! thou clod!
Thou fireless mixture of Earth's coldest clay!
Thou crazy dotard, crusted o'er with age
As thick as ice upon a standing pool!
Thou shrunken, sapless, wizen Grasshopper,
Consuming the green promise of my youth!
Go, get thee gone, and evil winds attend thee,
Thou antidote to love! thou bane of Hope,
Which like the float o' th' fisher's rod buoys up
The sinking line and by its fluctuations
Shows when the pang of Disappointment gnaws
Beneath it! But to me are both unknown:
I never more can hope and therefore never
Can suffer Disappointment.
He bears a charmed life and will outlast me
In mustiness of dry longevity,
Like some tough mummy wither'd, not decay'd—
His years are countless as the dusty race
That people an old Cheese and flourish only
In the unsoundest parts on't.
The big waves shatter thy frail skiff! the winds
Sing anything but lullabies unto thee!
The dark-hair'd Midnight grant no ray to thee,
But that of lightning, or the dreadful splendour

Of the conflicting wave! the red bolt scathe thee!
Why was I link'd with such a frowzy mate,
With such a fusty partner of my days?

*   *   *

ACT I, SC. V

[Amoret *finds that the* Devil *has been enjoined by her husband to guard her in his absence.*]

*   *   *

AMORET.   Alas!
Am I entrusted then to thee?
   DEVIL.   Dost weep?
Is that a tear which stains thy cheek? Nay—now
It quivers at the tip-end of thy nose
Which makes it somewhat dubious from which feature
It first had issue.
   AMORET.   I conjure thee—
   DEVIL.   Tears!
The rain of sentiment, the dews of feeling,
The beads of sensibility!
They are the coinage of a single wish.
I know that ye can summon them at will.
They are a woman's weapons, sword and shield,
Wherewith she braves remonstrance and breaks hearts—
Those faithful sluices never are drawn dry.
Even the withering heat of passion
But leads them forth in greater plenitude.
What! more! I know ye can command them, woman,
Even to the precise number, ten or twenty,
As suits occasion—
More yet? Methinks the cavity o' thy skull
Is brine i' th' room o' brains. More yet? at this rate

You'd float a ship o' the line.
This is the cogent stream wherewith ye turn
The mill-wheel of men's love (whose motion
Guides all the inner workings o' the heart)
And grind what grist ye please.
 AMORET. I pray thee—
 DEVIL. Get thee to bed—yet stay—but one
  word more—
Let there be no somnambulations,
No colloquy of soft-tongued whisperings
Like the low hum of the delighted bee
I' th' calyx of a lily—no kerchief-waving!
No footfalls i' th' still night! Lie quietly,
Without the movement of one naughty muscle,
Still as a kernel in its stone, and lifeless
As the dull yoke within its parent shell,
Ere yet the *punctum saliens* vivify it.
I know ye are perverse, and ever wish,
Maugre my wholesome admonitions,
To run obliquely like the bishop at chess,
But I'll cry 'check' to ye, I warrant ye,
I'll prove a 'stalemate' to ye.

* * *

ACT III, SC. II

[Magus *returning finds that the* Devil, *the better to guard his charge, has disguised himself as* Amoret.]

OUTSIDE OF THE COTTAGE—EARLY MORNING

* * *

 MAGUS. I do much fear my Devil hath play'd false
Or that the weeds of wanton Idleness
Have mantled his clear wit. Why comes he not?

* * *

(Enter DEVIL, *still veil'd)*
Ha! Amoret, awake, abroad so early
Blanching the roses of thy cheeks. What now!
The gray cock hath not crow'd, the glow-worm still
Leads on unpal'd his train of emerald light.
   DEVIL. Good faith, most venerable necromancer,
The roses of my visage are not blanch'd
But rather have attain'd (be thou my judge)
Unto a depth of dusky colouring.
(Unveils)
  MAGUS. How now, my Hellish Minister, dark child
Of bottomless Hades; what rude waggery,
What jejune undigested joke is this,
To quilt thy fuscous haunches with the flounc'd,
Frilled, finical delicacy of female dress?
How hast thou dar'd to girdle thy brown sides
And prop thy monstrous vertebrae with stays?
Speak out, thou petticoated Solecism,
Thou hairy trifler! what mad pranks have sent
Thy diabolical wits a-wool-gathering?
   DEVIL. A-linen-gathering I grant you, Master.
  MAGUS. Certes, it seems your Devilship to-night
Is unaccountably facetious!
Speak and beware the magic of my spells!
Or I will rive yon mighty Cedar-Tree
Sheer from its topmost windiest branch unto
The lowest fang o' th' root—between each half
I'll place thy sinful carcase and again
When the cleft stem shall close without a fissure
Thy bunching body shall be quash'd as flat
As spider in a hinge.

*   *   *

ACT III, SC. II

[Magus *recounts to the* Devil *his unsuccessful journey.*]

* * *

MAGUS. Half the powers o' th' other world
Were leagued against my journeying: but had not
The irresistible and lawless might
Of brazen-handed fix'd Fatality
Oppos'd me, I had done it. The black storm,
From out whose mass of volum'd vapour sprang
The lively curling thunderbolt, had ceas'd
Long ere from out the dewy depth of Pines
Emerging on the hollow'd banks, that bound
The leapings of the saucy tide, I stood—
The mighty waste of moaning waters lay
So goldenly in moonlight, whose clear lamp
With its long line of vibratory lustre
Trembled on the dun surface, that my Spirit
Was buoyant with rejoicings. Each hoar wave
With crisped undulation arching rose,
Thence falling in white ridge with sinuous slope
Dash'd headlong to the shore and spread along
The sands its tender fringe of creamy spray.
Thereat my shallop lightly I unbound,
Spread my white sail and rode exulting on
The placid murmurings of each feathery wave
That hurried into sparkles round the cleaving
Of my dark Prow; but scarcely had I past
The third white line of breakers when a squall
Fell on me from the North, an inky Congress
O' the Republican clouds unto the zenith
Rush'd from th' horizon upwards with the speed

Of their own thunder-bolts.
The seas divided and dim Phantasies
Came thronging thickly round me, with hot eyes
Unutterable things came flitting by me;
Semblance of palpability was in them,
Albeit the wavering lightnings glitter'd thro'
Their shadow'd immaterialities.
Black shapes clung to my boat; a sullen owl
Perch'd on the Prow, and overhead the hum
As of infernal Spirits in mid Heaven
Holding aerial council caught mine ear.
Then came a band of melancholy sprites,
White as their shrouds and motionlessly pale
Like some young Ashwood when the argent Moon
Looks in upon its many silver stems:
And thrice my name was syllabled i' th' air
And thrice upon the wave, like that loud voice
Which thro' the deep dark night i' th' olden time
Came sounding o'er the lone Ionian.
Thereat I girded round my loins the scarf
Thy Mother Hecate gave me and withstood
The violent tempest: the insulting surge
Rode over me in glassy arch but dar'd not
Sprinkle one drop of its nefarious spray
Upon my charmed person: the red heralds
O' th' heavy-footed thunder glanc'd beside me,
Kiss'd my bar'd front and curl'd around my brow
In lambent wreaths of circling fire, but could not
Singe one loose lock of vagrant grey, that floated
To the wind's dalliance. But nor magic spells,
Vigour of heart or vigilance of hand,
Could back the Ocean's spumy menacings,

Which drove my leaky skiff upon the sands.
Soon as I touch'd firm Earth, each mounting billow
Fell laxly back into its windless bed,
And all the moon-lit Ocean slumber'd still.
Thrice with bold prow I breasted the rough spume,
But thrice a vitreous wall of waves up sprung
Ridging the level sea—so far'd it with me
Foil'd of my purpose. Some unwholesome star,
Some spells of darker Gramarie than mine,
Rul'd the dim night and would not grant me passage.

* * *

CLARIBEL
A MELODY

I

WHERE Claribel low-lieth
    The breezes pause and die,
        Letting the rose-leaves fall:
But the solemn oak-tree sigheth,
    Thick-leaved, ambrosial,
    With an ancient melody
    Of an inward agony,
Where Claribel low-lieth.

II

At eve the beetle boometh
    Athwart the thicket lone:
At noon the wild bee hummeth
    About the moss'd headstone:
At midnight the moon cometh,
    And looketh down alone.

Her song the lintwhite swelleth,
The clear-voiced mavis dwelleth,
  The callow throstle lispeth,
The slumbrous wave outwelleth,
  The babbling runnel crispeth,
The hollow grot replieth
  Where Claribel low-lieth.

SUPPOSED CONFESSIONS OF A SECOND-RATE SENSITIVE MIND

*   *   *

WHY not believe then? Why not yet
Anchor thy frailty there, where man
Hath moor'd and rested? Ask the sea
At midnight, when the crisp slope waves
After a tempest, rib and fret
The broad-imbased beach, why he
Slumbers not like a mountain tarn?
Wherefore his ridges are not curls
And ripples of an inland mere?
Wherefore he moaneth thus, nor can
Draw down into his vexed pools
All that blue heaven which hues and paves
The other? I am too forlorn,
Too shaken: my own weakness fools
My judgment, and my spirit whirls,
Moved from beneath with doubt and fear.

*   *   *

          For the Ox
Feeds in the herb, and sleeps, or fills

The horned valleys all about,
And hollows of the fringed hills
In summer heats, with placid lows
Unfearing, till his own blood flows
About his hoof. And in the flocks
The lamb rejoiceth in the year,
And raceth freely with his fere,
And answers to his mother's calls
From the flower'd furrow. In a time,
Of which he wots not, run short pains
Thro' his warm heart; and then, from whence
He knows not, on his light there falls
A shadow; and his native slope,
Where he was wont to leap and climb,
Floats from his sick and filmed eyes,
And something in the darkness draws
His forehead earthward, and he dies.

* * *

            Oh teach me yet
Somewhat before the heavy clod
Weighs on me, and the busy fret
Of that sharp-headed worm begins
In the gross blackness underneath.

O weary life! O weary death!
O spirit and heart made desolate!
O damned vacillating state!

MARIANA

> Mariana in the moated grange.
> *Measure for Measure.*

With blackest moss the flower-plots
    Were thickly crusted, one and all:
    The rusted nails fell from the knots
That held the pear to the gable-wall.
The broken sheds look'd sad and strange:
    Unlifted was the clinking latch;
    Weeded and worn the ancient thatch
Upon the lonely moated grange.
        She only said, 'My life is dreary,
           He cometh not', she said;
        She said, 'I am aweary, aweary,
           I would that I were dead!'

Her tears fell with the dews at even;
    Her tears fell ere the dews were dried;
She could not look on the sweet heaven,
    Either at morn or eventide.
After the flitting of the bats,
    When thickest dark did trance the sky,
    She drew her casement-curtain by,
And glanced athwart the glooming flats.
        She only said, 'The night is dreary,
           He cometh not', she said;
        She said, 'I am aweary, aweary,
           I would that I were dead!'

Upon the middle of the night,
    Waking she heard the night-fowl crow:

The cock sung out an hour ere light:
  From the dark fen the oxen's low
Came to her: without hope of change,
  In sleep she seem'd to walk forlorn,
  Till cold winds woke the gray-eyed morn
About the lonely moated grange.
    She only said, 'The day is dreary,
      He cometh not', she said;
    She said, 'I am aweary, aweary,
      I would that I were dead!'

About a stone-cast from the wall
  A sluice with blacken'd waters slept,
And o'er it many, round and small,
  The cluster'd marish-mosses crept.
Hard by a poplar shook alway,
  All silver-green with gnarled bark:
  For leagues no other tree did mark
The level waste, the rounding gray.
    She only said, 'My life is dreary,
      He cometh not', she said;
    She said, 'I am aweary, aweary,
      I would that I were dead!'

And ever when the moon was low,
  And the shrill winds were up and away,
In the white curtain, to and fro,
  She saw the gusty shadow sway.
But when the moon was very low,
  And wild winds bound within their cell,
  The shadow of the poplar fell
Upon her bed, across her brow.

> She only said, 'The night is dreary,
>   He cometh not', she said;
> She said, 'I am aweary, aweary,
>   I would that I were dead!'

All day within the dreamy house,
  The doors upon their hinges creak'd;
The blue fly sung in the pane; the mouse
  Behind the mouldering wainscot shriek'd,
Or from the crevice peer'd about.
  Old faces glimmer'd thro' the doors,
  Old footsteps trod the upper floors,
Old voices called her from without.
> She only said, 'My life is dreary,
>   He cometh not', she said;
> She said, 'I am aweary, aweary,
>   I would that I were dead!'

The sparrow's chirrup on the roof,
  The slow clock ticking, and the sound
Which to the wooing wind aloof
  The poplar made, did all confound
Her sense; but most she loathed the hour
  When the thick-moted sunbeam lay
  Athwart the chambers, and the day
Was sloping toward his western bower.
> Then, said she, 'I am very dreary,
>   He will not come', she said;
> She wept, 'I am aweary, aweary,
>   Oh God, that I were dead!'

TO ——

* * *

Like that strange angel which of old,
 Until the breaking of the light,
Wrestled with wandering Israel,
 Past Yabbok brook the livelong night,
And heaven's mazed signs stood still
In the dim tract of Penuel.

ODE TO MEMORY

IV

Come forth, I charge thee, arise,
 Thou of the many tongues, the myriad eyes!
 Thou comest not with shows of flaunting vines
  Unto mine inner eye,
  Divinest Memory!
Thou wert not nursed by the waterfall
Which ever sounds and shines
 A pillar of white light upon the wall
Of purple cliffs, aloof descried:
Come from the woods that belt the gray hill-side,
 The seven elms, the poplars four
 That stand beside my father's door,
And chiefly from the brook that loves
To purl o'er matted cress and ribbed sand,
Or dimple in the dark of rushy coves,
Drawing into his narrow earthen urn,
 In every elbow and turn,
The filter'd tribute of the rough woodland,
 O! hither lead thy feet!

Pour round mine ears the livelong bleat
Of the thick-fleeced sheep from wattled folds,
    Upon the ridged wolds,
When the first matin-song hath waken'd loud
Over the dark dewy earth forlorn,
What time the amber morn
Forth gushes from beneath a low-hung cloud.

*   *   *

SONG

I

A SPIRIT haunts the year's last hours
    Dwelling amid these yellowing bowers:
    To himself he talks;
For at eventide, listening earnestly,
At his work you may hear him sob and sigh
    In the walks;
    Earthward he boweth the heavy stalks
Of the mouldering flowers:
    Heavily hangs the broad sunflower
        Over its grave i' the earth so chilly;
    Heavily hangs the hollyhock,
        Heavily hangs the tiger-lily.

II

The air is damp, and hush'd, and close,
As a sick man's room when he taketh repose
    An hour before death;
My very heart faints and my whole soul grieves
At the moist rich smell of the rotting leaves,
    And the breath
    Of the fading edges of box beneath,
And the year's last rose.

Heavily hangs the broad sunflower
   Over its grave i' the earth so chilly;
Heavily hangs the hollyhock,
   Heavily hangs the tiger-lily.

A CHARACTER

With a half-glance upon the sky
At night he said, 'The wanderings
Of this most intricate Universe
Teach me the nothingness of things'.
Yet could not all creation pierce
Beyond the bottom of his eye.

He spake of beauty: that the dull
Saw no divinity in grass,
Life in dead stones, or spirit in air;
Then looking as 'twere in a glass,
He smooth'd his chin and sleek'd his hair,
And said the earth was beautiful.

He spake of virtue: not the gods
More purely, when they wish to charm
Pallas and Juno sitting by:
And with a sweeping of the arm,
And a lack-lustre dead-blue eye,
Devolved his rounded periods.

Most delicately hour by hour
He canvass'd human mysteries,
And trod on silk, as if the winds
Blew his own praises in his eyes,
And stood aloof from other minds
In impotence of fancied power.

With lips depress'd as he were meek,
Himself unto himself he sold:
Upon himself himself did feed:
Quiet, dispassionate, and cold,
And other than his form of creed,
With chisell'd features clear and sleek.

THE DYING SWAN

I

THE plain was grassy, wild and bare,
    Wide, wild and open to the air,
    Which had built up everywhere
An under-roof of doleful gray.
With an inner voice the river ran,
Adown it floated a dying swan,
    And loudly did lament.
It was the middle of the day.
Ever the weary wind went on,
    And took the reed-tops as it went.

II

Some blue peaks in the distance rose,
And white against the cold-white sky,
Shone out their crowning snows.
  One willow over the river wept,
And shook the wave as the wind did sigh;
Above in the wind was the swallow,
    Chasing itself at its own wild will,
    And far thro' the marish green and still
    The tangled water-courses slept,
Shot over with purple, and green, and yellow.

III

The wild swan's death-hymn took the soul
Of that waste place with joy
Hidden in sorrow: at first to the ear
The warble was low, and full and clear;
And floating about the under-sky,
Prevailing in weakness, the coronach stole
Sometimes afar, and sometimes anear;
But anon her awful jubilant voice,
With a music strange and manifold,
Flow'd forth on a carol free and bold;
As when a mighty people rejoice
With shawms, and with cymbals, and harps of gold,
And the tumult of their acclaim is roll'd
Thro' the open gates of the city afar,
To the shepherd who watcheth the evening star.
And the creeping mosses and clambering weeds,
And the willow-branches hoar and dank,
And the wavy swell of the soughing reeds,
And the wave-worn horns of the echoing bank,
And the silvery marish-flowers that throng
The desolate creeks and pools among,
Were flooded over with eddying song.

A DIRGE

I

Now is done thy long day's work;
Fold thy palms across thy breast,
Fold thine arms, turn to thy rest.
    Let them rave.

Shadows of the silver birk
Sweep the green that folds thy grave.
    Let them rave.

II

Thee nor carketh care nor slander;
Nothing but the small cold worm
Fretteth thine enshrouded form.
    Let them rave.
Light and shadow ever wander
O'er the green that folds thy grave.
    Let them rave.

III

Thou wilt not turn upon thy bed;
Chaunteth not the brooding bee
Sweeter tones than calumny?
    Let them rave.
Thou wilt never raise thine head
From the green that folds thy grave.
    Let them rave.

IV

Crocodiles wept tears for thee;
The woodbine and eglatere
Drip sweeter dews than traitor's tear.
    Let them rave.
Rain makes music in the tree
O'er the green that folds thy grave.
    Let them rave.

V

Round thee blow, self-pleached deep,
Bramble roses, faint and pale,
And long purples of the dale.
    Let them rave.
These in every shower creep
Thro' the green that folds thy grave.
    Let them rave.

VI

The gold-eyed kingcups fine;
The frail bluebell peereth over
Rare broidry of the purple clover.
    Let them rave.
Kings have no such couch as thine,
As the green that folds thy grave.
    Let them rave.

VII

Wild words wander here and there:
God's great gift of speech abused
Makes thy memory confused:
    But let them rave.
The balm-cricket carols clear
In the green that folds thy grave.
    Let them rave.

LISETTE

MY light Lisette
  Is grave and shrewd,
  And half a prude,
And half coquette.

So staid and set,
   So terse and trim,
   So arch and prim,
Is my Lisette.

A something settled and precise
Has made a home in both the eyes
      Of my Lisette,
Lives in the little wilful hands,
   The little foot that glides and flits
Braced with dark silken sandal-bands,
   Even in the coxcomb parrokette
That on the drooping shoulder sits
      Of trim Lisette.

The measured motion of the blood,
   The words, where each one tells,
Too logical for womanhood,
   Brief changes rung on silver bells:
The cheek with health's close kisses warm,
   The finished form so light,
Such fullness in a little form
   As satisfies the sight:
The bodice fitted so exact,
   The nutbrown tress so crisply curled,
And the whole woman so compact,
   Her match is nowhere in the world:
Such knowledge of the modes of life,
   And household order such,
As might create a perfect wife,
   Not careful overmuch:

All these so moved me
  When we met,
I would she loved me,
  Trim Lisette.

What if to-morrow morn I go,
  And in an accent clipt and clear
  Say some three words within her ear?—
I think she would not answer 'No'.
  But by the ribbon in her hair,
  And those untasted lips, I swear,
    I keep some little doubt as yet;
      With such an eye,
      So grave and sly,
        Looks my Lisette.
      What words may show
      The 'Yes', the 'No'
        Of trim Lisette?
      The doubt is less,
        Since last we met;
      Let it be 'Yes',
        My sweet Lisette.

MILTON'S MULBERRY

Look what love the puddle-pated square-caps have for me!
I am Milton's Mulberry, Milton's, Milton's Mulberry,
But they whip't and rusticated him who planted me,
Milton's, Milton's Mulberry, Milton's, Milton's Mulberry!
Old and hollow, somewhat crooked in the shoulders as you
  see,

Full of summer foliage yet, but propped and padded curiously,
I would sooner have been planted by the hand that planted me
Than have grown in Paradise and dropped my fruit on
    Adam's knee.
Look what love the tiny-witted Trenchers have for me!

THE LADY OF SHALOTT

PART I

On either side the river lie
    Long fields of barley and of rye,
    That clothe the wold and meet the sky;
And thro' the field the road runs by
    To many-tower'd Camelot;
And up and down the people go,
Gazing where the lilies blow
Round an island there below,
    The island of Shalott.

Willows whiten, aspens quiver,
Little breezes dusk and shiver
Thro' the wave that runs for ever
By the island in the river
    Flowing down to Camelot.
Four gray walls, and four gray towers,
Overlook a space of flowers,
And the silent isle imbowers
    The Lady of Shalott.

By the margin, willow-veil'd,
Slide the heavy barges trail'd

By slow horses; and unhail'd
The shallop flitteth silken-sail'd
　　　Skimming down to Camelot:
But who hath seen her wave her hand?
Or at the casement seen her stand?
Or is she known in all the land,
　　　The Lady of Shalott?

Only reapers, reaping early
In among the bearded barley,
Hear a song that echoes cheerly
From the river winding clearly,
　　　Down to tower'd Camelot:
And by the moon the reaper weary,
Piling sheaves in uplands airy,
Listening, whispers ''Tis the fairy
　　　Lady of Shalott'.

PART II

There she weaves by night and day
A magic web with colours gay.
She has heard a whisper say,
A curse is on her if she stay
　　　To look down to Camelot.
She knows not what the curse may be,
And so she weaveth steadily,
And little other care hath she,
　　　The Lady of Shalott.

And moving thro' a mirror clear
That hangs before her all the year,
Shadows of the world appear.
There she sees the highway near
　　　Winding down to Camelot:

There the river eddy whirls,
And there the surly village-churls,
And the red cloaks of market girls,
    Pass onward from Shalott.

Sometimes a troop of damsels glad,
An abbot on an ambling pad,
Sometimes a curly shepherd-lad,
Or long-hair'd page in crimson clad,
    Goes by to tower'd Camelot;
And sometimes thro' the mirror blue
The knights come riding two and two:
She hath no loyal knight and true,
    The Lady of Shalott.

But in her web she still delights
To weave the mirror's magic sights,
For often thro' the silent nights
A funeral, with plumes and lights
    And music, went to Camelot:
Or when the moon was overhead,
Came two young lovers lately wed;
'I am half sick of shadows', said
    The Lady of Shalott.

PART III

A bow-shot from her bower-eaves,
He rode between the barley-sheaves,
The sun came dazzling thro' the leaves,
And flamed upon the brazen greaves
    Of bold Sir Lancelot.

A red-cross knight for ever kneel'd
To a lady in his shield,
That sparkled on the yellow field,
    Beside remote Shalott.

The gemmy bridle glitter'd free,
Like to some branch of stars we see
Hung in the golden Galaxy.
The bridle bells rang merrily
    As he rode down to Camelot:
And from his blazon'd baldric slung
A mighty silver bugle hung,
And as he rode his armour rung,
    Beside remote Shalott.

All in the blue unclouded weather
Thick-jewell'd shone the saddle-leather,
The helmet and the helmet-feather
Burn'd like one burning flame together,
    As he rode down to Camelot.
As often thro' the purple night,
Below the starry clusters bright,
Some bearded meteor, trailing light,
    Moves over still Shalott.

His broad clear brow in sunlight glow'd;
On burnish'd hooves his war-horse trode;
From underneath his helmet flow'd
His coal-black curls as on he rode,
    As he rode down to Camelot.
From the bank and from the river
He flash'd into the crystal mirror,
'Tirra lirra', by the river
    Sang Sir Lancelot.

She left the web, she left the loom,
She made three paces thro' the room,
She saw the water-lily bloom,
She saw the helmet and the plume,
    She look'd down to Camelot.
Out flew the web and floated wide;
The mirror crack'd from side to side;
'The curse is come upon me', cried
    The Lady of Shalott.

PART IV

In the stormy east-wind straining,
The pale yellow woods were waning,
The broad stream in his banks complaining,
Heavily the low sky raining
    Over tower'd Camelot;
Down she came and found a boat
Beneath a willow left afloat,
And round about the prow she wrote
    The Lady of Shalott.

And down the river's dim expanse
Like some bold seër in a trance,
Seeing all his own mischance—
With a glassy countenance
    Did she look to Camelot.
And at the closing of the day
She loosed the chain, and down she lay;
The broad stream bore her far away,
    The Lady of Shalott.

Lying, robed in snowy white
That loosely flew to left and right—

The leaves upon her falling light—
Thro' the noises of the night
     She floated down to Camelot:
And as the boat-head wound along
The willowy hills and fields among,
They heard her singing her last song,
     The Lady of Shalott.

Heard a carol, mournful, holy,
Chanted loudly, chanted lowly,
Till her blood was frozen slowly,
And her eyes were darken'd wholly,
     Turn'd to tower'd Camelot.
For ere she reach'd upon the tide
The first house by the water-side,
Singing in her song she died,
     The Lady of Shalott.

Under tower and balcony,
By garden-wall and gallery,
A gleaming shape she floated by,
Dead-pale between the houses high,
     Silent into Camelot.
Out upon the wharfs they came,
Knight and burgher, lord and dame,
And round the prow they read her name,
     The Lady of Shalott.

Who is this? and what is here?
And in the lighted palace near
Died the sound of royal cheer;
And they cross'd themselves for fear,
     All the knights at Camelot:

But Lancelot mused a little space;
He said, 'She has a lovely face;
God in his mercy lend her grace,
    The Lady of Shalott'.

THE TWO VOICES

A still small voice spake unto me,
  'Thou art so full of misery,
  Were it not better not to be?'

Then to the still small voice I said;
'Let me not cast in endless shade
What is so wonderfully made'.

To which the voice did urge reply;
'To-day I saw the dragon-fly
Come from the wells where he did lie.

'An inner impulse rent the veil
Of his old husk: from head to tail
Came out clear plates of sapphire mail.

'He dried his wings: like gauze they grew;
Thro' crofts and pastures wet with dew
A living flash of light he flew'.

    *   *   *

I wept, 'Tho' I should die, I know
That all about the thorn will blow
In tufts of rosy-tinted snow;

'And men, thro' novel spheres of thought
Still moving after truth long sought,
Will learn new things when I am not'.

'Yet', said the secret voice, 'some time,
Sooner or later, will gray prime
Make thy grass hoar with early rime.

'Not less swift souls that yearn for light,
Rapt after heaven's starry flight,
Would sweep the tracts of day and night.

'Not less the bee would range her cells,
The furzy prickle fire the dells,
The foxglove cluster dappled bells'.

* * *

'Do men love thee? Art thou so bound
To men, that how thy name may sound
Will vex thee lying underground?

'The memory of the wither'd leaf
In endless time is scarce more brief
Than of the garner'd Autumn-sheaf.

'Go, vexed Spirit, sleep in trust;
The right ear, that is fill'd with dust,
Hears little of the false or just'.

* * *

'Consider well', the voice replied,
'His face, that two hours since hath died;
Wilt thou find passion, pain or pride?

'Will he obey when one commands?
Or answer should one press his hands?
He answers not, nor understands.

'His palms are folded on his breast:
There is no other thing express'd
But long disquiet merged in rest.

'His lips are very mild and meek:
Tho' one should smite him on the cheek,
And on the mouth, he will not speak.

'His little daughter, whose sweet face
He kiss'd, taking his last embrace,
Becomes dishonour to her race—

'His sons grow up that bear his name,
Some grow to honour, some to shame,—
But he is chill to praise or blame.

'He will not hear the north-wind rave,
Nor, moaning, household shelter crave
From winter rains that beat his grave.

'High up the vapours fold and swim:
About him broods the twilight dim:
The place he knew forgetteth him'.

* * *

THE MILLER'S DAUGHTER

* * *

ARISE, and let us wander forth,
 To yon old mill across the wolds;
 For look, the sunset, south and north,
Winds all the vale in rosy folds,
And fires your narrow casement glass,
 Touching the sullen pool below:
On the chalk-hill the bearded grass
 Is dry and dewless. Let us go.

FATIMA

O LOVE, Love, Love! O withering might!
O sun, that from thy noonday height
Shudderest when I strain my sight,
Throbbing thro' all thy heat and light,
  Lo, falling from my constant mind,
  Lo, parch'd and wither'd, deaf and blind,
  I whirl like leaves in roaring wind.

Last night I wasted hateful hours
Below the city's eastern towers:
I thirsted for the brooks, the showers:
I roll'd among the tender flowers:
  I crush'd them on my breast, my mouth;
  I look'd athwart the burning drouth
  Of that long desert to the south.

Last night, when some one spoke his name,
From my swift blood that went and came
A thousand little shafts of flame
Were shiver'd in my narrow frame.
  O Love, O fire! once he drew
  With one long kiss my whole soul thro'
  My lips, as sunlight drinketh dew.

Before he mounts the hill, I know
He cometh quickly: from below
Sweet gales, as from deep gardens, blow
Before him, striking on my brow.
  In my dry brain my spirit soon,
  Down-deepening from swoon to swoon,
  Faints like a dazzled morning moon.

The wind sounds like a silver wire,
And from beyond the noon a fire
Is pour'd upon the hills, and nigher
The skies stoop down in their desire;
    And, isled in sudden seas of light,
    My heart, pierced thro' with fierce delight,
    Bursts into blossom in his sight.

My whole soul waiting silently,
All naked in a sultry sky,
Droops blinded with his shining eye:
I *will* possess him or will die.
    I will grow round him in his place,
    Grow, live, die looking on his face,
    Die, dying clasp'd in his embrace.

ŒNONE

THERE lies a vale in Ida, lovelier
    Than all the valleys of Ionian hills.
    The swimming vapour slopes athwart the glen,
Puts forth an arm, and creeps from pine to pine,
And loiters, slowly drawn. On either hand
The lawns and meadow-ledges midway down
Hang rich in flowers, and far below them roars
The long brook falling thro' the clov'n ravine
In cataract after cataract to the sea.
Behind the valley topmost Gargarus
Stands up and takes the morning: but in front
The gorges, opening wide apart, reveal
Troas and Ilion's column'd citadel,
The crown of Troas.

                    Hither came at noon
Mournful Œnone, wandering forlorn
Of Paris, once her playmate on the hills.
Her cheek had lost the rose, and round her neck
Floated her hair or seem'd to float in rest.
She, leaning on a fragment twined with vine,
Sang to the stillness, till the mountain-shade
Sloped downward to her seat from the upper cliff.

'O mother Ida, many-fountain'd Ida,
Dear mother Ida, harken ere I die.
For now the noonday quiet holds the hill:
The grasshopper is silent in the grass:
The lizard, with his shadow on the stone,
Rests like a shadow, and the winds are dead.
The purple flower droops: the golden bee
Is lily-cradled: I alone awake.
My eyes are full of tears, my heart of love,
My heart is breaking, and my eyes are dim,
And I am all aweary of my life.

'O mother Ida, many-fountain'd Ida,
Dear mother Ida, harken ere I die.
Hear me, O Earth, hear me, O Hills, O Caves
That house the cold crown'd snake! O mountain brooks,
I am the daughter of a River-God,
Hear me, for I will speak and build up all
My sorrow with my song, as yonder walls
Rose slowly to a music slowly breathed,
A cloud that gather'd shape: for it may be
That, while I speak of it, a little while
My heart may wander from its deeper woe.

'O mother Ida, many-fountain'd Ida,
Dear mother Ida, harken ere I die.
I waited underneath the dawning hills,
Aloft the mountain lawn was dewy dark,
And dewy dark aloft the mountain pine:
Beautiful Paris, evil-hearted Paris,
Leading a jet-black goat white-horn'd, white-hooved,
Came up from reedy Simois all alone.

'O mother Ida, harken ere I die.
Far-off the torrent call'd me from the cleft:
Far up the solitary morning smote
The streaks of virgin snow. With down-dropt eyes
I sat alone: white-breasted like a star
Fronting the dawn he moved; a leopard skin
Droop'd from his shoulder, but his sunny hair
Cluster'd about his temples like a God's:
And his cheek brighten'd as the foam-bow brightens
When the wind blows the foam, and all my heart
Went forth to embrace him coming ere he came.

'Dear mother Ida, harken ere I die.
He smiled, and opening out his milk-white palm
Disclosed a fruit of pure Hesperian gold,
That smelt ambrosially, and while I look'd
And listen'd, the full-flowing river of speech
Came down upon my heart.
                      '"My own Œnone,
Beautiful-brow'd Œnone, my own soul,
Behold this fruit, whose gleaming rind ingrav'n
'For the most fair', would seem to award it thine,
As lovelier than whatever Oread haunt

The knolls of Ida, loveliest in all grace
Of movement, and the charm of married brows."

'Dear mother Ida, harken ere I die.
He prest the blossom of his lips to mine,
And added "This was cast upon the board,
When all the full-faced presence of the Gods
Ranged in the halls of Peleus; whereupon
Rose feud, with question unto whom 'twere due:
But light-foot Iris brought it yester-eve,
Delivering, that to me, by common voice
Elected umpire, Herè comes to-day,
Pallas and Aphroditè, claiming each
This meed of fairest. Thou, within the cave
Behind yon whispering tuft of oldest pine,
Mayst well behold them unbeheld, unheard
Hear all, and see thy Paris judge of Gods".

'Dear mother Ida, harken ere I die.
It was the deep midnoon: one silvery cloud
Had lost his way between the piney sides
Of this long glen. Then to the bower they came,
Naked they came to that smooth-swarded bower,
And at their feet the crocus brake like fire,
Violet, amaracus, and asphodel,
Lotos and lilies: and a wind arose,
And overhead the wandering ivy and vine,
This way and that, in many a wild festoon
Ran riot, garlanding the gnarled boughs
With bunch and berry and flower thro' and thro'.

'O mother Ida, harken ere I die.
On the tree-tops a crested peacock lit,

And o'er him flow'd a golden cloud, and lean'd
Upon him, slowly dropping fragrant dew.
Then first I heard the voice of her, to whom
Coming thro' Heaven, like a light that grows
Larger and clearer, with one mind the Gods
Rise up for reverence. She to Paris made
Proffer of royal power, ample rule
Unquestion'd, overflowing revenue
Wherewith to embellish state, "from many a vale
And river-sunder'd champaign clothed with corn,
Or labour'd mine undrainable of ore.
Honour", she said, "and homage, tax and toll,
From many an inland town and haven large,
Mast-throng'd beneath her shadowing citadel
In glassy bays among her tallest towers".

'O mother Ida, harken ere I die.
Still she spake on and still she spake of power,
"Which in all action is the end of all;
Power fitted to the season; wisdom-bred
And throned of wisdom—from all neighbour crowns
Alliance and allegiance, till thy hand
Fail from the sceptre-staff. Such boon from me,
From me, Heaven's Queen, Paris, to thee king-born,
A shepherd all thy life but yet king-born,
Should come most welcome, seeing men, in power
Only, are likest gods, who have attain'd
Rest in a happy place and quiet seats
Above the thunder, with undying bliss
In knowledge of their own supremacy".

'Dear mother Ida, harken ere I die.
She ceased, and Paris held the costly fruit

Out at arm's-length, so much the thought of power
Flatter'd his spirit; but Pallas where she stood
Somewhat apart, her clear and bared limbs
O'erthwarted with the brazen-headed spear
Upon her pearly shoulder leaning cold,
The while, above, her full and earnest eye
Over her snow-cold breast and angry cheek
Kept watch, waiting decision, made reply.

'"Self-reverence, self-knowledge, self-control,
These three alone lead life to sovereign power.
Yet not for power (power of herself
Would come uncall'd for) but to live by law,
Acting the law we live by without fear;
And, because right is right, to follow right
Were wisdom in the scorn of consequence."

'Dear mother Ida, harken ere I die.
Again she said: "I woo thee not with gifts.
Sequel of guerdon could not alter me
To fairer. Judge thou me by what I am,
So shalt thou find me fairest.
      Yet, indeed,
If gazing on divinity disrobed
Thy mortal eyes are frail to judge of fair,
Unbias'd by self-profit, oh! rest thee sure
That I shall love thee well and cleave to thee,
So that my vigour, wedded to thy blood,
Shall strike within thy pulses, like a God's,
To push thee forward thro' a life of shocks,
Dangers, and deeds, until endurance grow
Sinew'd with action, and the full-grown will,

Circled thro' all experiences, pure law,
Commeasure perfect freedom".
       'Here she ceas'd,
And Paris ponder'd, and I cried, "O Paris,
Give it to Pallas!" but he heard me not,
Or hearing would not hear me, woe is me!

 'O mother Ida, many-fountain'd Ida,
Dear mother Ida, harken ere I die.
Idalian Aphroditè beautiful,
Fresh as the foam, new-bathed in Paphian wells,
With rosy slender fingers backward drew
From her warm brows and bosom her deep hair
Ambrosial, golden round her lucid throat
And shoulder: from the violets her light foot
Shone rosy-white, and o'er her rounded form
Between the shadows of the vine-bunches
Floated the glowing sunlights, as she moved.

 'Dear mother Ida, harken ere I die.
She with a subtle smile in her mild eyes,
The herald of her triumph, drawing nigh
Half-whisper'd in his ear, "I promise thee
The fairest and most loving wife in Greece",
She spoke and laugh'd: I shut my sight for fear:
But when I look'd, Paris had raised his arm,
And I beheld great Herè's angry eyes,
As she withdrew into the golden cloud,
And I was left alone within the bower;
And from that time to this I am alone,
And I shall be alone until I die.

 'Yet, mother Ida, harken ere I die.
Fairest—why fairest wife? am I not fair?

My love hath told me so a thousand times.
Methinks I must be fair, for yesterday,
When I past by, a wild and wanton pard,
Eyed like the evening star, with playful tail
Crouch'd fawning in the weed. Most loving is she?
Ah me, my mountain shepherd, that my arms
Were wound about thee, and my hot lips prest
Close, close to thine in that quick-falling dew
Of fruitful kisses, thick as Autumn rains
Flash in the pools of whirling Simois.

'O mother, hear me yet before I die.
They came, they cut away my tallest pines,
My tall dark pines, that plumed the craggy ledge
High over the blue gorge, and all between
The snowy peak and snow-white cataract
Foster'd the callow eaglet—from beneath
Whose thick mysterious boughs in the dark morn
The panther's roar came muffled, while I sat
Low in the valley. Never, never more
Shall lone Œnone see the morning mist
Sweep thro' them; never see them overlaid
With narrow moon-lit slips of silver cloud,
Between the loud stream and the trembling stars.

'O mother, hear me yet before I die.
I wish that somewhere in the ruin'd folds,
Among the fragments tumbled from the glens,
Or the dry thickets, I could meet with her
The Abominable, that uninvited came
Into the fair Peleïan banquet-hall,
And cast the golden fruit upon the board,
And bred this change; that I might speak my mind,

And tell her to her face how much I hate
Her presence, hated both of Gods and men.

  'O mother, hear me yet before I die.
Hath he not sworn his love a thousand times,
In this green valley, under this green hill,
Ev'n on this hand, and sitting on this stone?
Seal'd it with kisses? water'd it with tears?
O happy tears, and how unlike to these!
O happy Heaven, how canst thou see my face?
O happy earth, how canst thou bear my weight?
O death, death, death, thou ever-floating cloud,
There are enough unhappy on this earth,
Pass by the happy souls, that love to live:
I pray thee, pass before my light of life,
And shadow all my soul, that I may die.
Thou weighest heavy on the heart within,
Weigh heavy on my eyelids: let me die.

  'O mother, hear me yet before I die.
I will not die alone, for fiery thoughts
Do shape themselves within me, more and more,
Whereof I catch the issue, as I hear
Dead sounds at night come from the inmost hills,
Like footsteps upon wool. I dimly see
My far-off doubtful purpose, as a mother
Conjectures of the features of her child
Ere it is born: her child!—a shudder comes
Across me: never child be born of me,
Unblest, to vex me with his father's eyes!

  'O mother, hear me yet before I die.
Hear me, O earth. I will not die alone,

Lest their shrill happy laughter come to me
Walking the cold and starless road of Death
Uncomforted, leaving my ancient love
With the Greek woman. I will rise and go
Down into Troy, and ere the stars come forth
Talk with the wild Cassandra, for she says
A fire dances before her, and a sound
Rings ever in her ears of armed men.
What this may be I know not, but I know
That, wheresoe'er I am by night and day,
All earth and air seem only burning fire.'

THE PALACE OF ART

I BUILT my soul a lordly pleasure-house,
    Wherein at ease for aye to dwell.
I said, 'O Soul, make merry and carouse,
    Dear soul, for all is well'.

A huge crag-platform, smooth as burnish'd brass
    I chose. The ranged ramparts bright
From level meadow-bases of deep grass
    Suddenly scaled the light.

Thereon I built it firm. Of ledge or shelf
    The rock rose clear, or winding stair.
My soul would live alone unto herself
    In her high palace there.

And 'while the world runs round and round', I said,
    'Reign thou apart, a quiet king,
Still as, while Saturn whirls, his stedfast shade
    Sleeps on his luminous ring'.

To which my soul made answer readily:
   'Trust me, in bliss I shall abide
In this great mansion, that is built for me,
    So royal-rich and wide'.

* * *
* * *

Four courts I made, East, West and South and North,
   In each a squared lawn, wherefrom
The golden gorge of dragons spouted forth
    A flood of fountain-foam.

And round the cool green courts there ran a row
   Of cloisters, branch'd like mighty woods,
Echoing all night to that sonorous flow
    Of spouted fountain-floods.

And round the roofs a gilded gallery
   That lent broad verge to distant lands,
Far as the wild swan wings, to where the sky
    Dipt down to sea and sands.

From those four jets four currents in one swell
   Across the mountain stream'd below
In misty folds, that floating as they fell
    Lit up a torrent-bow.

And high on every peak a statue seem'd
   To hang on tiptoe, tossing up
A cloud of incense of all odour steam'd
    From out a golden cup.

So that she thought, 'And who shall gaze upon
   My palace with unblinded eyes,
While this great bow will waver in the sun,
    And that sweet incense rise?'

For that sweet incense rose and never fail'd,
   And, while day sank or mounted higher,
The light aërial gallery, golden-rail'd,
     Burnt like a fringe of fire.

Likewise the deep-set windows, stain'd and traced,
   Would seem slow-flaming crimson fires
From shadow'd grots of arches interlaced,
     And tipt with frost-like spires.

* * *
* * *

Full of long-sounding corridors it was,
   That over-vaulted grateful gloom,
Thro' which the livelong day my soul did pass,
     Well-pleased, from room to room.

Full of great rooms and small the palace stood,
   All various, each a perfect whole
From living Nature, fit for every mood
     And change of my still soul.

For some were hung with arras green and blue,
   Showing a gaudy summer-morn,
Where with puff'd cheek the belted hunter blew
     His wreathed bugle-horn.

One seem'd all dark and red—a tract of sand,
   And some one pacing there alone,
Who paced for ever in a glimmering land,
     Lit with a low large moon.

One show'd an iron coast and angry waves.
   You seem'd to hear them climb and fall
And roar rock-thwarted under bellowing caves,
     Beneath the windy wall.

And one, a full-fed river winding slow
   By herds upon an endless plain,
The ragged rims of thunder brooding low,
      With shadow-streaks of rain.

And one, the reapers at their sultry toil.
   In front they bound the sheaves. Behind
Were realms of upland, prodigal in oil,
      And hoary to the wind.

And one a foreground black with stones and slags,
   Beyond, a line of heights, and higher
All barr'd with long white cloud the scornful crags,
      And highest, snow and fire.

And one, an English home—gray twilight pour'd
   On dewy pastures, dewy trees,
Softer than sleep—all things in order stored,
      A haunt of ancient Peace.

Nor these alone, but every landscape fair,
   As fit for every mood of mind,
Or gay, or grave, or sweet, or stern, was there
      Not less than truth design'd.

* * *
* * *

Or the maid-mother by a crucifix,
   In tracts of pasture sunny-warm,
Beneath branch-work of costly sardonyx
      Sat smiling, babe in arm.

Or in a clear-wall'd city on the sea,
   Near gilded organ-pipes, her hair
Wound with white roses, slept St Cecily;
      An angel look'd at her.

Or thronging all one porch of Paradise
   A group of Houris bow'd to see
The dying Islamite, with hands and eyes
     That said, We wait for thee.

Or mythic Uther's deeply-wounded son
   In some fair space of sloping greens
Lay, dozing in the vale of Avalon,
     And watch'd by weeping queens.

Or hollowing one hand against his ear,
   To list a foot-fall, ere he saw
The wood-nymph, stay'd the Ausonian king to hear
     Of wisdom and of law.

Or over hills with peaky tops engrail'd,
   And many a tract of palm and rice,
The throne of Indian Cama slowly sail'd
     A summer fann'd with spice.

Or sweet Europa's mantle blew unclasp'd,
   From off her shoulder backward borne:
From one hand droop'd a crocus: one hand grasp'd
     The mild bull's golden horn.

Or else flush'd Ganymede, his rosy thigh
   Half buried in the Eagle's down,
Sole as a flying star shot thro' the sky
     Above the pillar'd town.

Nor these alone: but every legend fair
   Which the supreme Caucasian mind
Carved out of Nature for itself, was there,
     Not less than life, design'd.

    *   *   *
    *   *   *

Then in the towers I placed great bells that swung,
    Moved of themselves, with silver sound;
And with choice paintings of wise men I hung
    The royal dais round.

For there was Milton like a seraph strong,
    Beside him Shakespeare bland and mild;
And there the world-worn Dante grasp'd his song,
    And somewhat grimly smiled.

And there the Ionian father of the rest;
    A million wrinkles carved his skin;
A hundred winters snow'd upon his breast,
    From cheek and throat and chin.

Above, the fair hall-ceiling stately-set
    Many an arch high up did lift,
And angels rising and descending met
    With interchange of gift.

Below was all mosaic choicely plann'd
    With cycles of the human tale
Of this wide world, the times of every land
    So wrought, they will not fail.

The people here, a beast of burden slow,
    Toil'd onward, prick'd with goads and stings;
Here play'd, a tiger, rolling to and fro
    The heads and crowns of kings;

Here rose, an athlete, strong to break or bind
    All force in bonds that might endure,
And here once more like some sick man declined,
    And trusted any cure.

But over these she trod: and those great bells
    Began to chime. She took her throne:
She sat betwixt the shining Oriels,
    To sing her songs alone.

And thro' the topmost Oriels' coloured flame
    Two godlike faces gazed below;
Plato the wise, and large-brow'd Verulam,
    The first of those who know.

And all those names, that in their motion were
    Full-welling fountain-heads of change,
Betwixt the slender shafts were blazon'd fair
    In diverse raiment strange:

Thro' which the lights, rose, amber, emerald, blue,
    Flush'd in her temples and her eyes,
And from her lips, as morn from Memnon, drew
    Rivers of melodies.

No nightingale delighteth to prolong
    Her low preamble all alone,
More than my soul to hear her echo'd song
    Throb thro' the ribbed stone;

Singing and murmuring in her feastful mirth,
    Joying to feel herself alive,
Lord over Nature, Lord of the visible earth,
    Lord of the senses five;

Communing with herself: 'All these are mine,
    And let the world have peace or wars,
'Tis one to me'. She—when young night divine
    Crown'd dying day with stars,

Making sweet close of his delicious toils—
    Lit light in wreaths and anadems,
And pure quintessences of precious oils
      In hollow'd moons of gems,

To mimic heaven; and clapt her hands and cried,
    'I marvel if my still delight
In this great house so royal-rich, and wide,
    Be flatter'd to the height.

'O all things fair to sate my various eyes!
    O shapes and hues that please me well!
O silent faces of the Great and Wise,
    My Gods, with whom I dwell!

'O God-like isolation which art mine,
    I can but count thee perfect gain,
What time I watch the darkening droves of swine
    That range on yonder plain.

'In filthy sloughs they roll a prurient skin,
    They graze and wallow, breed and sleep;
And oft some brainless devil enters in,
    And drives them to the deep'.

Then of the moral instinct would she prate
    And of the rising from the dead,
As hers by right of full-accomplish'd Fate;
    And at the last she said:

'I take possession of man's mind and deed.
    I care not what the sects may brawl.
I sit as God holding no form of creed,
    But contemplating all'.

* * *

Full oft the riddle of the painful earth
    Flash'd thro' her as she sat alone,
Yet not the less held she her solemn mirth,
        And intellectual throne.

And so she throve and prosper'd: so three years
    She prosper'd: on the fourth she fell,
Like Herod, when the shout was in his ears,
        Struck thro' with pangs of hell.

Lest she should fail and perish utterly,
    God, before whom ever lie bare
The abysmal deeps of Personality,
        Plagued her with sore despair.

When she would think, where'er she turn'd her sight
    The airy hand confusion wrought,
Wrote, 'Mene, mene', and divided quite
        The kingdom of her thought.

Deep dread and loathing of her solitude
    Fell on her, from which mood was born
Scorn of herself; again, from out that mood
        Laughter at her self-scorn.

'What! is not this my place of strength', she said,
    'My spacious mansion built for me,
Whereof the strong foundation-stones were laid
        Since my first memory?'

But in dark corners of her palace stood
    Uncertain shapes; and unawares
On white-eyed phantasms weeping tears of blood,
        And horrible nightmares,

And hollow shades enclosing hearts of flame,
    And, with dim fretted foreheads all,
On corpses three-months-old at noon she came,
    That stood against the wall.

A spot of dull stagnation, without light
    Or power of movement, seem'd my soul,
'Mid onward-sloping motions infinite
    Making for one sure goal.

A still salt pool, lock'd in with bars of sand,
    Left on the shore; that hears all night
The plunging seas draw backward from the land
    Their moon-led waters white.

A star that with the choral starry dance
    Join'd not, but stood, and standing saw
The hollow orb of moving Circumstance
    Roll'd round by one fix'd law.

Back on herself her serpent pride had curl'd.
    'No voice,' she shriek'd in that lone hall,
'No voice breaks thro' the stillness of this world:
    One deep, deep silence all!'

She, mouldering with the dull earth's mouldering sod,
    Inwrapt tenfold in slothful shame,
Lay there exiled from eternal God,
    Lost to her place and name;

And death and life she hated equally,
    And nothing saw, for her despair,
But dreadful time, dreadful eternity,
    No comfort anywhere;

Remaining utterly confused with fears,
   And ever worse with growing time,
And ever unrelieved by dismal tears,
     And all alone in crime:

Shut up as in a crumbling tomb, girt round
   With blackness as a solid wall,
Far off she seem'd to hear the dully sound
     Of human footsteps fall.

As in strange lands a traveller walking slow,
   In doubt and great perplexity,
A little before moon-rise hears the low
     Moan of an unknown sea;

And knows not if it be thunder, or a sound
   Of rocks thrown down, or one deep cry
Of great wild beasts; then thinketh, 'I have found
     A new land, but I die.'

She howl'd aloud, 'I am on fire within.
   There comes no murmur of reply.
What is it that will take away my sin,
     And save me lest I die?'

So when four years were wholly finished,
   She threw her royal robes away.
'Make me a cottage in the vale', she said,
     'Where I may mourn and pray.

'Yet pull not down my palace towers, that are
   So lightly, beautifully built:
Perchance I may return with others there
     When I have purged my guilt.'

THE MAY QUEEN

* * *

When the flowers come again, mother, beneath the waning light
    You'll never see me more in the long gray fields at night;
When from the dry dark wold the summer airs blow cool
On the oat-grass and the sword-grass, and the bulrush in the pool.

* * *

THE LOTOS-EATERS

'Courage!' he said, and pointed toward the land,
    'This mounting wave will roll us shoreward soon.'
    In the afternoon they came unto a land
In which it seemed always afternoon.
All round the coast the languid air did swoon,
Breathing like one that hath a weary dream.
Full-faced above the valley stood the moon;
And like a downward smoke, the slender stream
Along the cliff to fall and pause and fall did seem.

A land of streams! some, like a downward smoke,
Slow-dropping veils of thinnest lawn, did go;
And some thro' wavering lights and shadows broke,
Rolling a slumbrous sheet of foam below.
They saw the gleaming river seaward flow
From the inner land: far off, three mountain-tops,
Three silent pinnacles of aged snow,
Stood sunset-flush'd: and, dew'd with showery drops,
Up-clomb the shadowy pine above the woven copse.

The charmed sunset linger'd low adown
In the red West: thro' mountain clefts the dale
Was seen far inland, and the yellow down
Border'd with palm, and many a winding vale
And meadow, set with slender galingale;
A land where all things always seem'd the same!
And round about the keel with faces pale,
Dark faces pale against that rosy flame,
The mild-eyed melancholy Lotos-eaters came.

Branches they bore of that enchanted stem,
Laden with flower and fruit, whereof they gave
To each, but whoso did receive of them,
And taste, to him the gushing of the wave
Far far away did seem to mourn and rave
On alien shores; and if his fellow spake,
His voice was thin, as voices from the grave;
And deep-asleep he seem'd, yet all awake,
And music in his ears his beating heart did make.

They sat them down upon the yellow sand,
Between the sun and moon upon the shore;
And sweet it was to dream of Fatherland,
Of child, and wife, and slave; but evermore
Most weary seem'd the sea, weary the oar,
Weary the wandering fields of barren foam.
Then some one said, 'We will return no more';
And all at once they sang, 'Our island home
Is far beyond the wave; we will no longer roam'.

CHORIC SONG

I

There is sweet music here that softer falls
Than petals from blown roses on the grass,
Or night-dews on still waters between walls
Of shadowy granite, in a gleaming pass;
Music that gentlier on the spirit lies,
Than tir'd eyelids upon tir'd eyes;
Music that brings sweet sleep down from the blissful skies.
Here are cool mosses deep,
And thro' the moss the ivies creep,
And in the stream the long-leaved flowers weep,
And from the craggy ledge the poppy hangs in sleep.

II

Why are we weigh'd upon with heaviness,
And utterly consumed with sharp distress,
While all things else have rest from weariness?
All things have rest: why should we toil alone,
We only toil, who are the first of things,
And make perpetual moan,
Still from one sorrow to another thrown:
Nor ever fold our wings,
And cease from wanderings,
Nor steep our brows in slumber's holy balm;
Nor harken what the inner spirit sings,
'There is no joy but calm!'—
Why should we only toil, the roof and crown of things?

III

Lo! in the middle of the wood,
The folded leaf is woo'd from out the bud
With winds upon the branch, and there
Grows green and broad, and takes no care,
Sun-steep'd at noon, and in the moon
Nightly dew-fed; and turning yellow
Falls, and floats adown the air.
Lo! sweeten'd with the summer light,
The full-juiced apple, waxing over-mellow,
Drops in a silent autumn night.
All its allotted length of days,
The flower ripens in its place,
Ripens and fades, and falls, and hath no toil,
Fast-rooted in the fruitful soil.

IV

Hateful is the dark-blue sky,
Vaulted o'er the dark-blue sea.
Death is the end of life; ah, why
Should life all labour be?
Let us alone. Time driveth onward fast,
And in a little while our lips are dumb.
Let us alone. What is it that will last?
All things are taken from us, and become
Portions and parcels of the dreadful Past.
Let us alone. What pleasure can we have
To war with evil? Is there any peace
In ever climbing up the climbing wave?
All things have rest, and ripen toward the grave
In silence; ripen, fall and cease:
Give us long rest or death, dark death, or dreamful ease.

V

How sweet it were, hearing the downward stream,
With half-shut eyes ever to seem
Falling asleep in a half-dream!
To dream and dream, like yonder amber light,
Which will not leave the myrrh-bush on the height;
To hear each other's whisper'd speech;
Eating the Lotos day by day,
To watch the crisping ripples on the beach,
And tender curving lines of creamy spray;
To lend our hearts and spirits wholly
To the influence of mild-minded melancholy;
To muse and brood and live again in memory,
With those old faces of our infancy
Heap'd over with a mound of grass,
Two handfuls of white dust, shut in an urn of brass!

VI

Dear is the memory of our wedded lives,
And dear the last embraces of our wives
And their warm tears: but all hath suffer'd change:
For surely now our household hearths are cold:
Our sons inherit us: our looks are strange:
And we should come like ghosts to trouble joy.
Or else the island princes over-bold
Have eat our substance, and the minstrel sings
Before them of the ten years' war in Troy,
And our great deeds, as half-forgotten things.
Is there confusion in the little isle?
Let what is broken so remain.
The Gods are hard to reconcile:
'Tis hard to settle order once again.

There *is* confusion worse than death,
Trouble on trouble, pain on pain,
Long labour unto aged breath,
Sore task to hearts worn out by many wars
And eyes grown dim with gazing on the pilot-stars.

VII

But, propt on beds of amaranth and moly,
How sweet (while warm airs lull us, blowing lowly)
With half-dropt eyelid still,
Beneath a heaven dark and holy,
To watch the long bright river drawing slowly
His waters from the purple hill—
To hear the dewy echoes calling
From cave to cave thro' the thick-twined vine—
To watch the emerald-colour'd water falling
Thro' many a wov'n acanthus-wreath divine!
Only to hear and see the far-off sparkling brine,
Only to hear were sweet, stretch'd out beneath the pine.

VIII

The Lotos blooms below the barren peak:
The Lotos blows by every winding creek:
All day the wind breathes low with mellower tone:
Thro' every hollow cave and alley lone
Round and round the spicy downs the yellow Lotos-dust is blown.
We have had enough of action, and of motion we,
Roll'd to starboard, roll'd to larboard, when the surge was seething free,
Where the wallowing monster spouted his foam-fountains in the sea.

Let us swear an oath, and keep it with an equal mind,
In the hollow Lotos-land to live and lie reclined
On the hills like Gods together, careless of mankind.
For they lie beside their nectar, and the bolts are hurl'd
Far below them in the valleys, and the clouds are lightly curl'd
Round their golden houses, girdled with the gleaming world:
Where they smile in secret, looking over wasted lands,
Blight and famine, plague and earthquake, roaring deeps and
    fiery sands,
Clanging fights, and flaming towns, and sinking ships, and
    praying hands.
But they smile, they find a music centred in a doleful song
Steaming up, a lamentation and an ancient tale of wrong,
Like a tale of little meaning tho' the words are strong;
Chanted from an ill-used race of men that cleave the soil,
Sow the seed, and reap the harvest with enduring toil,
Storing yearly little dues of wheat, and wine and oil;
Till they perish and they suffer—some, 'tis whisper'd—down
    in hell
Suffer endless anguish, others in Elysian valleys dwell,
Resting weary limbs at last on beds of asphodel.
Surely, surely, slumber is more sweet than toil, the shore
Than labour in the deep mid-ocean, wind and wave and oar;
Oh rest ye, brother mariners, we will not wander more.

A DREAM OF FAIR WOMEN

I READ, before my eyelids dropt their shade,
  '*The Legend of Good Women*', long ago
Sung by the morning star of song, who made
  His music heard below;

Dan Chaucer, the first warbler, whose sweet breath
   Preluded those melodious bursts that fill
The spacious times of great Elizabeth
   With sounds that echo still.

And, for a while, the knowledge of his art
   Held me above the subject, as strong gales
Hold swollen clouds from raining, tho' my heart,
   Brimful of those wild tales,

Charged both mine eyes with tears. In every land
   I saw, wherever light illumineth,
Beauty and anguish walking hand in hand
   The downward slope to death.

Those far-renowned brides of ancient song
   Peopled the hollow dark, like burning stars,
And I heard sounds of insult, shame, and wrong,
   And trumpets blown for wars;

And clattering flints batter'd with clanging hoofs;
   And I saw crowds in column'd sanctuaries;
And forms that pass'd at windows and on roofs
   Of marble palaces;

Corpses across the threshold; heroes tall
   Dislodging pinnacle and parapet
Upon the tortoise creeping to the wall;
   Lances in ambush set;

And high shrine-doors burst thro' with heated blasts
   That run before the fluttering tongues of fire;
White surf wind-scatter'd over sails and masts,
   And ever climbing higher;

Squadrons and squares of men in brazen plates,
  Scaffolds, still sheets of water, divers woes,
Ranges of glimmering vaults with iron grates,
  And hush'd seraglios.

So shape chased shape as swift as, when to land
  Bluster the winds and tides the self-same way,
Crisp foam-flakes scud along the level sand,
  Torn from the fringe of spray.

I started once, or seem'd to start in pain,
  Resolved on noble things, and strove to speak,
As when a great thought strikes along the brain,
  And flushes all the cheek.

And once my arm was lifted to hew down
  A cavalier from off his saddle-bow,
That bore a lady from a leaguer'd town;
  And then, I know not how,

All those sharp fancies, by down-lapsing thought
  Stream'd onward, lost their edges, and did creep
Roll'd on each other, rounded, smooth'd, and brought
  Into the gulfs of sleep.

At last methought that I had wander'd far
  In an old wood: fresh-wash'd in coolest dew
The maiden splendours of the morning star
  Shook in the stedfast blue.

Enormous elm-tree-boles did stoop and lean
  Upon the dusky brushwood underneath
Their broad curved branches, fledged with clearest green,
  New from its silken sheath.

The dim red morn had died, her journey done,
  And with dead lips smiled at the twilight plain,
Half-fall'n across the threshold of the sun,
  Never to rise again.

There was no motion in the dumb dead air,
  Not any song of bird or sound of rill;
Gross darkness of the inner sepulchre
  Is not so deadly still

As that wide forest. Growths of jasmine turn'd
  Their humid arms festooning tree to tree,
And at the root thro' lush green grasses burn'd
  The red anemone.

I knew the flowers, I knew the leaves, I knew
  The tearful glimmer of the languid dawn
On those long, rank, dark wood-walks drench'd in dew,
  Leading from lawn to lawn.

The smell of violets, hidden in the green,
  Pour'd back into my empty soul and frame
The times when I remember to have been
  Joyful and free from blame.

And from within me a clear under-tone
  Thrill'd thro' mine ears in that unblissful clime,
'Pass freely thro': the wood is all thine own,
  Until the end of time'.

At length I saw a lady within call,
  Stiller than chisell'd marble, standing there;
A daughter of the gods, divinely tall,
  And most divinely fair.

Her loveliness with shame and with surprise
    Froze my swift speech: she turning on my face
The star-like sorrows of immortal eyes,
    Spoke slowly in her place.

'I had great beauty: ask thou not my name:
    No one can be more wise then destiny.
Many drew swords and died. Where'er I came
    I brought calamity.'

'No marvel, sovereign lady: in fair field
    Myself for such a face had boldly died,'
I answer'd free; and turning I appeal'd
    To one that stood beside.

But she, with sick and scornful looks averse,
    To her full height her stately stature draws;
'My youth', she said, 'was blasted with a curse:
    This woman was the cause.

'I was cut off from hope in that sad place,
    Which men call'd Aulis in those iron years:
My father held his hand upon his face;
    I, blinded with my tears,

'Still strove to speak: my voice was thick with sighs
    As in a dream. Dimly I could descry
The stern black-bearded kings with wolfish eyes,
    Waiting to see me die.

'The high masts flicker'd as they lay afloat;
    The crowds, the temples, waver'd, and the shore;
The bright death quiver'd at the victim's throat;
    Touch'd; and I knew no more.'

Whereto the other with a downward brow:
  'I would the white cold heavy-plunging foam,
Whirl'd by the wind, had roll'd me deep below,
  Then when I left my home'.

Her slow full words sank thro' the silence drear,
  As thunder-drops fall on a sleeping sea:
Sudden I heard a voice that cried, 'Come here,
  That I may look on thee'.

I turning saw, throned on a flowery rise,
  One sitting on a crimson scarf unroll'd;
A queen, with swarthy cheeks and bold black eyes,
  Brow-bound with burning gold.

She, flashing forth a haughty smile, began:
  'I govern'd men by change, and so I sway'd
All moods. 'Tis long since I have seen a man.
  Once, like the moon, I made

'The ever-shifting currents of the blood
  According to my humour ebb and flow.
I have no men to govern in this wood:
  That makes my only woe.

'Nay—yet it chafes me that I could not bend
  One will; nor tame and tutor with mine eye
That dull cold-blooded Cæsar. Prythee, friend,
  Where is Mark Antony?

'The man, my lover, with whom I rode sublime
  On Fortune's neck: we sat as God by God:
The Nilus would have risen before his time
  And flooded at our nod.

'We drank the Libyan Sun to sleep, and lit
    Lamps which out-burn'd Canopus. O my life
In Egypt! O the dalliance and the wit,
    The flattery and the strife,

'And the wild kiss, when fresh from war's alarms,
    My Hercules, my Roman Antony,
My mailed Bacchus leapt into my arms,
    Contented there to die!

'And there he died: and when I heard my name
    Sigh'd forth with life I would not brook my fear
Of the other: with a worm I balk'd his fame.
    What else was left? look here!'

(With that she tore her robe apart, and half
    The polish'd argent of her breast to sight
Laid bare. Thereto she pointed with a laugh,
    Showing the aspick's bite.)

'I died a Queen. The Roman soldier found
    Me lying dead, my crown about my brows,
A name for ever!—lying robed and crown'd,
    Worthy a Roman spouse.'

Her warbling voice, a lyre of widest range
    Struck by all passion, did fall down and glance
From tone to tone, and glided thro' all change
    Of liveliest utterance.

When she made pause I knew not for delight;
    Because with sudden motion from the ground
She raised her piercing orbs, and fill'd with light
    The interval of sound.

Still with their fires Love tipt his keenest darts;
　　As once they drew into two burning rings
All beams of Love, melting the mighty hearts
　　Of captains and of kings.

Slowly my sense undazzled. Then I heard
　　A noise of some one coming thro' the lawn
And singing clearer than the crested bird
　　That claps his wings at dawn.

'The torrent brooks of hallow'd Israel
　　From craggy hollows pouring, late and soon,
Sound all night long, in falling thro' the dell,
　　Far-heard beneath the moon.

'The balmy moon of blessed Israel
　　Floods all the deep-blue gloom with beams divine:
All night the splinter'd crags that wall the dell
　　With spires of silver shine.'

As one that museth where broad sunshine laves
　　The lawn by some cathedral, thro' the door
Hearing the holy organ rolling waves
　　Of sound on roof and floor

Within, and anthem sung, is charm'd and tied
　　To where he stands,—so stood I, when that flow
Of music left the lips of her that died
　　To save her father's vow;

The daughter of the warrior Gileadite,
　　A maiden pure; as when she went along
From Mizpeh's tower'd gate with welcome light,
　　With timbrel and with song.

My words leapt forth: 'Heaven heads the count of crimes
   With that wild oath'. She render'd answer high:
'Not so, nor once alone; a thousand times
   I would be born and die.

'Single I grew, like some green plant, whose root
   Creeps to the garden water-pipes beneath,
Feeding the flower; but ere my flower to fruit
   Changed, I was ripe for death.

'My God, my land, my father—these did move
   Me from my bliss of life, that Nature gave,
Lower'd softly with a threefold cord of love
   Down to a silent grave.

'And I went mourning, "No fair Hebrew boy
   Shall smile away my maiden blame among
The Hebrew mothers"—emptied of all joy,
   Leaving the dance and song,

'Leaving the olive-gardens far below,
   Leaving the promise of my bridal bower,
The valleys of grape-loaded vines that glow
   Beneath the battled tower.

'The light white cloud swam over us. Anon
   We heard the lion roaring from his den;
We saw the large white stars rise one by one,
   Or, from the darken'd glen,

'Saw God divide the night with flying flame,
   And thunder on the everlasting hills.
I heard Him, for He spake, and grief became
   A solemn scorn of ills.

'When the next moon was roll'd into the sky,
    Strength came to me that equall'd my desire.
How beautiful a thing it was to die
    For God and for my sire!

'It comforts me in this one thought to dwell,
    That I subdued me to my father's will;
Because the kiss he gave me, ere I fell,
    Sweetens the spirit still.

'Moreover it is written that my race
    Hew'd Ammon, hip and thigh, from Aroer
On Arnon unto Minneth'. Here her face
    Glow'd, as I look'd at her.

She lock'd her lips: she left me where I stood:
    'Glory to God', she sang, and past afar,
Thridding the sombre boskage of the wood,
    Toward the morning-star.

Losing her carol I stood pensively,
    As one that from a casement leans his head,
When midnight bells cease ringing suddenly,
    And the old year is dead.

'Alas! alas!' a low voice, full of care,
    Murmur'd beside me: 'Turn and look on me:
I am that Rosamond, whom men call fair,
    If what I was I be.

'Would I had been some maiden coarse and poor!
    O me, that I should ever see the light!
Those dragon eyes of anger'd Eleanor
    Do hunt me, day and night'.

She ceased in tears, fallen from hope and trust:
   To whom the Egyptian: 'O, you tamely died!
You should have clung to Fulvia's waist, and thrust
   The dagger thro' her side'.

With that sharp sound the white dawn's creeping beams,
   Stol'n to my brain, dissolved the mystery
Of folded sleep. The captain of my dreams
   Ruled in the eastern sky.

Morn broaden'd on the borders of the dark,
   Ere I saw her, who clasp'd in her last trance
Her murder'd father's head, or Joan of Arc,
   A light of ancient France;

Or her who knew that Love can vanquish Death,
   Who kneeling, with one arm about her king,
Drew forth the poison with her balmy breath,
   Sweet as new buds in Spring.

No memory labours longer from the deep
   Gold-mines of thought to lift the hidden ore
That glimpses, moving up, than I from sleep
   To gather and tell o'er

Each little sound and sight. With what dull pain
   Compass'd, how eagerly I sought to strike
Into that wondrous track of dreams again!
   But no two dreams are like.

As when a soul laments, which hath been blest,
   Desiring what is mingled with past years,
In yearnings that can never be exprest
   By signs or groans or tears;

Because all words, tho' cull'd with choicest art,
    Failing to give the bitter of the sweet,
Wither beneath the palate, and the heart
    Faints, faded by its heat.

TO J. S.

THE wind, that beats the mountain, blows
    More softly round the open wold,
And gently comes the world to those
    That are cast in gentle mould.

And me this knowledge bolder made,
    Or else I had not dared to flow
In these words toward you, and invade
    Even with a verse your holy woe.

'Tis strange that those we lean on most,
    Those in whose laps our limbs are nursed,
Fall into shadow, soonest lost:
    Those we love first are taken first.

God gives us love. Something to love
    He lends us; but, when love is grown
To ripeness, that on which it throve
    Falls off, and love is left alone.

This is the curse of time. Alas!
    In grief I am not all unlearn'd;
Once thro' mine own doors Death did pass;
    One went, who never hath return'd.

He will not smile—not speak to me
    Once more. Two years his chair is seen
Empty before us. That was he
    Without whose life I had not been.

Your loss is rarer; for this star
    Rose with you thro' a little arc
Of heaven, nor having wander'd far
    Shot on the sudden into dark.

I knew your brother: his mute dust
    I honour and his living worth:
A man more pure and bold and just
    Was never born into the earth.

I have not look'd upon you nigh,
    Since that dear soul hath fall'n asleep.
Great Nature is more wise than I:
    I will not tell you not to weep.

And tho' mine own eyes fill with dew,
    Drawn from the spirit thro' the brain,
I will not even preach to you,
    'Weep, weeping dulls the inward pain'.

Let Grief be her own mistress still.
    She loveth her own anguish deep
More than much pleasure. Let her will
    Be done—to weep or not to weep.

I will not say, 'God's ordinance
    Of Death is blown in every wind';
For that is not a common chance
    That takes away a noble mind.

His memory long will live alone
    In all our hearts, as mournful light
That broods above the fallen sun,
    And dwells in heaven half the night.

Vain solace! Memory standing near
    Cast down her eyes, and in her throat
Her voice seem'd distant, and a tear
    Dropt on the letters as I wrote.

I wrote I know not what. In truth,
    How *should* I soothe you anyway,
Who miss the brother of your youth?
    Yet something I did wish to say:

For he too was a friend to me:
    Both are my friends, and my true breast
Bleedeth for both; yet it may be
    That only silence suiteth best.

Words weaker than your grief would make
    Grief more. 'Twere better I should cease
Although myself could almost take
    The place of him that sleeps in peace.

Sleep sweetly, tender heart, in peace:
    Sleep, holy spirit, blessed soul,
While the stars burn, the moons increase,
    And the great ages onward roll.

Sleep till the end, true soul and sweet.
    Nothing comes to thee new or strange.
Sleep full of rest from head to feet;
    Lie still, dry dust, secure of change.

ON A MOURNER

I

Nature, so far as in her lies,
   Imitates God, and turns her face
   To every land beneath the skies,
Counts nothing that she meets with base,
But lives and loves in every place;

II

Fills out the homely quickset-screens,
   And makes the purple lilac ripe,
Steps from her airy hill, and greens
   The swamp, where humm'd the dropping snipe,
   With moss and braided marish-pipe;

III

And on thy heart a finger lays,
   Saying, 'Beat quicker, for the time
Is pleasant, and the woods and ways
   Are pleasant, and the beech and lime
   Put forth and feel a gladder clime'.

IV

And murmurs of a deeper voice,
   Going before to some far shrine,
Teach that sick heart the stronger choice,
   Till all thy life one way incline
   With one wide Will that closes thine.

V

And when the zoning eve has died
   Where yon dark valleys wind forlorn,
Come Hope and Memory, spouse and bride,
   From out the borders of the morn,
   With that fair child betwixt them born.

VI
And when no mortal motion jars
  The blackness round the tombing sod,
Thro' silence and the trembling stars
  Comes Faith from tracts no feet have trod,
  And Virtue, like a household god

VII
Promising empire: such as those
  Once heard at dead of night to greet
Troy's wandering prince, so that he rose
  With sacrifice, while all the fleet
  Had rest by stony hills of Crete.

'LOVE THOU THY LAND'

*   *   *

EV'N now we hear with inward strife
  A motion toiling in the gloom—
  The Spirit of the years to come
Yearning to mix himself with Life.

*   *   *

THE LOVER'S TALE

*   *   *

                  So I wove
Ev'n the dull-blooded poppy-stem, 'whose flower,
Hued with the scarlet of a fierce sunrise,
Like to the wild youth of an evil prince,
Is without sweetness, but who crowns himself
Above the naked poisons of his heart
In his old age'.

*   *   *

And first the chillness of the sprinkled brook
Smote on my brows, and then I seem'd to hear
Its murmur, as the drowning seaman hears,
Who with his head below the surface dropt
Listens the muffled booming indistinct
Of the confused floods, and dimly knows
His head shall rise no more.

* * *

SONNET

How thought you that this thing could captivate?
    What are those graces that could make her dear,
    Who is not worth the notice of a sneer,
To rouse the vapid devil of her hate?
A speech conventional, so void of weight
    That after it has buzzed about one's ear,
    'Twere rich refreshment for a week to hear
The dentist babble or the barber prate—

A hand displayed with many a little art,
    An eye that glances on her neighbour's dress,
    A foot too often shown for my regard,
An angel's form, a waiting-woman's heart,
    A perfect-featured face, expressionless,
    Insipid, as a Queen upon a card.

MORTE D'ARTHUR

So all day long the noise of battle roll'd
    Among the mountains by the winter sea;
    Until King Arthur's table, man by man,
Had fallen in Lyonnesse about their Lord,

King Arthur: then, because his wound was deep,
The bold Sir Bedivere uplifted him,
Sir Bedivere, the last of all his knights,
And bore him to a chapel nigh the field,
A broken chancel with a broken cross,
That stood on a dark strait of barren land.
On one side lay the Ocean, and on one
Lay a great water, and the moon was full.
   Then spake King Arthur to Sir Bedivere:
'The sequel of to-day unsolders all
The goodliest fellowship of famous knights
Whereof this world holds record. Such a sleep
They sleep—the men I loved. I think that we
Shall never more, at any future time,
Delight our souls with talk of knightly deeds,
Walking about the gardens and the halls
Of Camelot, as in the days that were.
I perish by this people which I made,—
Tho' Merlin sware that I should come again
To rule once more—but let what will be, be,
I am so deeply smitten thro' the helm
That without help I cannot last till morn.
Thou therefore take by brand Excalibur,
Which was my pride: for thou rememberest how
In those old days, one summer noon, an arm
Rose up from out the bosom of the lake,
Clothed in white samite, mystic, wonderful,
Holding the sword—and how I row'd across
And took it, and have worn it, like a king:
And, wheresoever I am sung or told
In aftertime, this also shall be known:
But now delay not: take Excalibur,

And fling him far into the middle mere:
Watch what thou seëst, and lightly bring me word'.
   To him replied the bold Sir Bedivere:
'It is not meet, Sir King, to leave thee thus,
Aidless, alone, and smitten thro' the helm.
A little thing may harm a wounded man.
Yet I thy hest will all perform at full,
Watch what I see, and lightly bring thee word'.
   So saying, from the ruin'd shrine he stept
And in the moon athwart the place of tombs,
Where lay the mighty bones of ancient men,
Old knights, and over them the sea-wind sang
Shrill, chill, with flakes of foam. He, stepping down
By zig-zag paths, and juts of pointed rock,
Came on the shining levels of the lake.
   There drew he forth the brand Excalibur,
And o'er him, drawing it, the winter moon,
Brightening the skirts of a long cloud, ran forth
And sparkled keen with frost against the hilt:
For all the haft twinkled with diamond sparks,
Myriads of topaz-lights, and jacinth-work
Of subtlest jewellery. He gazed so long
That both his eyes were dazzled, as he stood,
This way and that dividing the swift mind,
In act to throw: but at the last it seem'd
Better to leave Excalibur conceal'd
There in the many-knotted waterflags,
That whistled stiff and dry about the marge.
So strode he back slow to the wounded King.
   Then spake King Arthur to Sir Bedivere:
'Hast thou perform'd my mission which I gave?
What is it thou hast seen? or what hast heard?'

   And answer made the bold Sir Bedivere:
'I heard the ripple washing in the reeds,
And the wild water lapping on the crag'.
   To whom replied King Arthur, faint and pale:
'Thou hast betray'd thy nature and thy name,
Not rendering true answer, as beseem'd
Thy fealty, nor like a noble knight:
For surer sign had follow'd, either hand,
Or voice, or else a motion of the mere.
This is a shameful thing, for men to lie.
Yet now, I charge thee, quickly go again
As thou art lief and dear, and do the thing
I bad thee, watch, and lightly bring me word'.
   Then went Sir Bedivere the second time
Across the ridge, and paced beside the mere,
Counting the dewy pebbles, fix'd in thought;
But when he saw the wonder of the hilt,
How curiously and strangely chased, he smote
His palms together, and he cried aloud,
   'And if indeed I cast the brand away,
Surely a precious thing, one worthy note,
Should thus be lost for ever from the earth,
Which might have pleased the eyes of many men.
What good should follow this, if this were done?
What harm, undone? deep harm to disobey,
Seeing obedience is the bond of rule.
Were it well to obey then, if a king demand
An act unprofitable, against himself?
The King is sick, and knows not what he does.
What record, or what relic of my lord
Should be to aftertime, but empty breath
And rumours of a doubt? but were this kept,

Stored in some treasure-house of mighty kings,
Some one might show it at a joust of arms,
Saying, "King Arthur's sword, Excalibur,
Wrought by the lonely maiden of the Lake.
Nine years she wrought it, sitting in the deeps
Upon the hidden bases of the hills".
So might some old man speak in the aftertime
To all the people, winning reverence.
But now much honour and much fame were lost'.

   So spake he, clouded with his own conceit,
And hid Excalibur the second time,
And so strode back slow to the wounded King.

   Then spoke King Arthur, breathing heavily:
'What is it thou hast seen? or what hast heard?'

   And answer made the bold Sir Bedivere:
'I heard the water lapping on the crag,
And the long ripple washing in the reeds'.

   To whom replied King Arthur, much in wrath:
'Ah, miserable and unkind, untrue,
Unknightly, traitor-hearted! Woe is me!
Authority forgets a dying king,
Laid widow'd of the power in his eye
That bow'd the will. I see thee what thou art,
For thou, the latest-left of all my knights,
In whom should meet the offices of all,
Thou wouldst betray me for the precious hilt;
Either from lust of gold, or like a girl
Valuing the giddy pleasure of the eyes.
Yet, for a man may fail in duty twice,
And the third time may prosper, get thee hence:
But, if thou spare to fling Excalibur,
I will arise and slay thee with my hands'.

    Then quickly rose Sir Bedivere, and ran,
And, leaping down the ridges lightly, plunged
Among the bulrush-beds, and clutch'd the sword,
And strongly wheel'd and threw it. The great brand
Made lightnings in the splendour of the moon,
And flashing round and round, and whirl'd in an arch,
Shot like a streamer of the northern morn,
Seen where the moving isles of winter shock
By night, with noises of the northern sea.
So flash'd and fell the brand Excalibur:
But ere he dipt the surface, rose an arm
Clothed in white samite, mystic, wonderful,
And caught him by the hilt, and brandish'd him
Three times, and drew him under in the mere.
And lightly went the other to the King.
    Then spoke King Arthur, drawing thicker breath:
'Now see I by thine eyes that this is done.
Speak out: what is it thou hast heard, or seen?'
    And answer made the bold Sir Bedivere:
'Sir King, I closed mine eyelids, lest the gems
Should blind my purpose, for I never saw,
Nor shall see, here or elsewhere, till I die,
Not tho' I live three lives of mortal men,
So great a miracle as yonder hilt.
Then with both hands I flung him, wheeling him;
But when I look'd again, behold an arm,
Clothed in white samite, mystic, wonderful,
That caught him by the hilt, and brandish'd him
Three times, and drew him under in the mere'.
    And answer made King Arthur, breathing hard:
'My end draws nigh; 'tis time that I were gone.
Make broad thy shoulders to receive my weight,

And bear me to the margin; yet I fear
My wound hath taken cold, and I shall die'.
So saying, from the pavement he half rose,
Slowly, with pain, reclining on his arm,
And looking wistfully with wide blue eyes
As in a picture. Him Sir Bedivere
Remorsefully regarded thro' his tears,
And would have spoken, but he found not words,
Then took with care, and kneeling on one knee,
O'er both his shoulders drew the languid hands,
And rising bore him thro' the place of tombs.

 But, as he walk'd, King Arthur panted hard,
Like one that feels a nightmare on his bed
When all the house is mute. So sigh'd the King,
Muttering and murmuring at his ear, 'Quick, quick!
I fear it is too late, and I shall die'.
But the other swiftly strode from ridge to ridge,
Clothed with his breath, and looking, as he walk'd,
Larger than human on the frozen hills.
He heard the deep behind him, and a cry
Before. His own thought drove him, like a goad.
Dry clash'd his harness in the icy caves
And barren chasms, and all to left and right
The bare black cliff clang'd round him, as he based
His feet on juts of slippery crag that rang
Sharp-smitten with the dint of armed heels—
And on a sudden, lo! the level lake,
And the long glories of the winter moon.

 Then saw they how there hove a dusky barge,
Dark as a funeral scarf from stem to stern,
Beneath them; and descending they were ware
That all the decks were dense with stately forms

Black-stoled, black-hooded, like a dream—by these
Three Queens with crowns of gold—and from them rose
A cry that shiver'd to the tingling stars,
And, as it were one voice, an agony
Of lamentation, like a wind, that shrills
All night in a waste land, where no one comes,
Or hath come, since the making of the world.

    Then murmur'd Arthur, 'Place me in the barge',
And to the barge they came. There those three Queens
Put forth their hands, and took the King, and wept.
But she, that rose the tallest of them all
And fairest, laid his head upon her lap,
And loosed the shatter'd casque, and chafed his hands,
And call'd him by his name, complaining loud,
And dropping bitter tears against his brow
Striped with dark blood: for all his face was white
And colourless, and like the wither'd moon
Smote by the fresh beam of the springing east;
And all his greaves and cuisses dash'd with drops
Of onset; and the light and lustrous curls—
That made his forehead like a rising sun
High from the daïs-throne—were parch'd with dust;
Or, clotted into points and hanging loose,
Mix'd with the knightly growth that fringed his lips.
So like a shatter'd column lay the King;
Not like that Arthur who, with lance in rest,
From spur to plume a star of tournament,
Shot thro' the lists at Camelot, and charged
Before the eyes of ladies and of kings.

    Then loudly cried the bold Sir Bedivere,
'Ah! my Lord Arthur, whither shall I go?
Where shall I hide my forehead and my eyes?

For now I see the true old times are dead,
When every morning brought a noble chance,
And every chance brought out a noble knight.
Such times have been not since the light that led
The holy Elders with the gift of myrrh.
But now the whole ROUND TABLE is dissolved
Which was an image of the mighty world;
And I, the last, go forth companionless,
And the days darken round me, and the years,
Among new men, strange faces, other minds'.

 And slowly answered Arthur from the barge:
'The old order changeth, yielding place to new,
And God fulfils Himself in many ways,
Lest one good custom should corrupt the world.
Comfort thyself: what comfort is in me?
I have lived my life, and that which I have done
May He within Himself make pure! but thou,
If thou shouldst never see my face again,
Pray for my soul. More things are wrought by prayer
Than this world dreams of. Wherefore, let thy voice
Rise like a fountain for me night and day.
For what are men better than sheep or goats
That nourish a blind life within the brain,
If, knowing God, they lift not hands of prayer
Both for themselves and those who call them friend?
For so the whole round earth is every way
Bound by gold chains about the feet of God.
But now farewell. I am going a long way
With these thou seëst—if indeed I go—
(For all my mind is clouded with a doubt)
To the island-valley of Avilion;
Where falls not hail, or rain, or any snow,

Nor ever wind blows loudly; but it lies
Deep-meadow'd, happy, fair with orchard-lawns
And bowery hollows crown'd with summer sea,
Where I will heal me of my grievous wound'.
 So said he, and the barge with oar and sail
Moved from the brink, like some full-breasted swan
That, fluting a wild carol ere her death,
Ruffles her pure cold plume, and takes the flood
With swarthy webs. Long stood Sir Bedivere
Revolving many memories, till the hull
Look'd one black dot against the verge of dawn,
And on the mere the wailing died away.

THE GARDENER'S DAUGHTER

* * *

NOT wholly in the busy world, nor quite
Beyond it, blooms the garden that I love.
News from the humming city comes to it
In sound of funeral or of marriage bells;
And, sitting muffled in dark leaves, you hear
The windy clanging of the minster clock;
Although between it and the garden lies
A league of grass, wash'd by a slow broad stream,
That, stirr'd with languid pulses of the oar,
Waves all its lazy lilies, and creeps on,
Barge-laden, to three arches of a bridge
Crown'd with the minster-towers.
                    The fields between
Are dewy-fresh, browsed by deep-udder'd kine,

And all about the large lime feathers low,
The lime a summer home of murmurous wings.

* * *

As tho' 'twere yesterday, as tho' it were
The hour just flown, that morn with all its sound,
(For those old Mays had thrice the life of these,)
Rings in mine ears. The steer forgot to graze,
And, where the hedge-row cuts the pathway, stood,
Leaning his horns into the neighbour field,
And lowing to his fellows. From the woods
Came voices of the well-contented doves.
The lark could scarce get out his notes for joy,
But shook his song together as he near'd
His happy home, the ground. To left and right,
The cuckoo told his name to all the hills;
The mellow ouzel fluted in the elm;
The redcap whistled; and the nightingale
Sang loud, as tho' he were the bird of day.

* * *

We reach'd a meadow slanting to the North;
Down which a well-worn pathway courted us
To one green wicket in a privet hedge;
This, yielding, gave into a grassy walk
Thro' crowded lilac-ambush trimly pruned;
And one warm gust, full-fed with perfume, blew
Beyond us, as we enter'd in the cool.
The garden stretches southward. In the midst
A cedar spread his dark-green layers of shade.
The garden-glasses glanced, and momently
The twinkling laurel scatter'd silver lights.

* * *

LOVE AND DUTY

*   *   *

      The trance gave way
To those caresses, when a hundred times
In that last kiss, which never was the last,
Farewell, like endless welcome, lived and died.
Then follow'd counsel, comfort, and the words
That make a man feel strong in speaking truth;
Till now the dark was worn, and overhead
The lights of sunset and of sunrise mix'd
In that brief night; the summer night, that paused
Among her stars to hear us; stars that hung
Love-charm'd to listen: all the wheels of Time
Spun round in station, but the end had come.
 O then like those, who clench their nerves to rush
Upon their dissolution, we two rose,
There—closing like an individual life—
In one blind cry of passion and of pain,
Like bitter accusation ev'n to death,
Caught up the whole of love and utter'd it,
And bade adieu for ever.
      Live—yet live—
Shall sharpest pathos blight us, knowing all
Life needs for life is possible to will?—
Live happy; tend thy flowers; be tended by
My blessing! Should my Shadow cross thy thoughts
Too sadly for their peace, remand it thou
For calmer hours to Memory's darkest hold,
If not to be forgotten—not at once—
Not all forgotten. Should it cross thy dreams,
O might it come like one that looks content,

With quiet eyes unfaithful to the truth,
And point thee forward to a distant light,
Or seem to lift a burthen from thy heart
And leave thee freër, till thou wake refresh'd
Then when the first low matin-chirp hath grown
Full quire, and morning driv'n her plow of pearl
Far furrowing into light the mounded rack,
Beyond the fair green field and eastern sea.

ULYSSES

It little profits that an idle king,
By this still hearth, among these barren crags,
Match'd with an aged wife, I mete and dole
Unequal laws unto a savage race,
That hoard, and sleep, and feed, and know not me.
I cannot rest from travel: I will drink
Life to the lees: all times I have enjoy'd
Greatly, have suffer'd greatly, both with those
That loved me, and alone; on shore, and when
Thro' scudding drifts the rainy Hyades
Vext the dim sea: I am become a name;
For always roaming with a hungry heart
Much have I seen and known; cities of men
And manners, climates, councils, governments,
Myself not least, but honour'd of them all;
And drunk delight of battle with my peers,
Far on the ringing plains of windy Troy.
I am a part of all that I have met;
Yet all experience is an arch wherethro'
Gleams that untravell'd world, whose margin fades
For ever and for ever when I move.

How dull it is to pause, to make an end,
To rust unburnish'd, not to shine in use!
As tho' to breathe were life. Life piled on life
Were all too little, and of one to me
Little remains: but every hour is saved
From that eternal silence, something more,
A bringer of new things; and vile it were
For some three suns to store and hoard myself,
And this gray spirit yearning in desire
To follow knowledge like a sinking star,
Beyond the utmost bound of human thought.

   This is my son, mine own Telemachus,
To whom I leave the sceptre and the isle—
Well-loved of me, discerning to fulfil
This labour, by slow prudence to make mild
A rugged people, and thro' soft degrees
Subdue them to the useful and the good.
Most blameless is he, centred in the sphere
Of common duties, decent not to fail
In offices of tenderness, and pay
Meet adoration to my household gods,
When I am gone. He works his work, I mine.

   There lies the port; the vessel puffs her sail:
There gloom the dark broad seas. My mariners,
Souls that have toil'd, and wrought and thought with me—
That ever with a frolic welcome took
The thunder and the sunshine, and opposed
Free hearts, free foreheads—you and I are old;
Old age hath yet his honour and his toil;
Death closes all: but something ere the end,
Some work of noble note, may yet be done,
Not unbecoming men that strove with Gods.

The lights begin to twinkle from the rocks:
The long day wanes: the slow moon climbs: the deep
Moans round with many voices. Come, my friends,
'Tis not too late to seek a newer world.
Push off, and sitting well in order smite
The sounding furrows; for my purpose holds
To sail beyond the sunset, and the baths
Of all the western stars, until I die.
It may be that the gulfs will wash us down:
It may be we shall touch the Happy Isles,
And see the great Achilles, whom we knew.
Tho' much is taken, much abides; and tho'
We are not now that strength which in old days
Moved earth and heaven; that which we are, we are;
One equal temper of heroic hearts,
Made weak by time and fate, but strong in will
To strive, to seek, to find, and not to yield.

TITHONUS

THE woods decay, the woods decay and fall,
The vapours weep their burthen to the ground,
Man comes and tills the field and lies beneath,
And after many a summer dies the swan.
Me only cruel immortality
Consumes: I wither slowly in thine arms,
Here at the quiet limit of the world,
A white-hair'd shadow roaming like a dream
The ever-silent spaces of the East,
Far-folded mists, and gleaming halls of morn.

  Alas! for this gray shadow, once a man—
So glorious in his beauty and thy choice,

Who madest him thy chosen, that he seem'd
To his great heart none other than a God!
I ask'd thee, 'Give me immortality'.
Then didst thou grant mine asking with a smile,
Like wealthy men who care not how they give.
But thy strong Hours indignant work'd their wills,
And beat me down and marr'd and wasted me,
And tho' they could not end me, left me maim'd
To dwell in presence of immortal youth,
Immortal age beside immortal youth,
And all I was, in ashes. Can thy love,
Thy beauty, make amends, tho' even now,
Close over us, the silver star, thy guide,
Shines in those tremulous eyes that fill with tears
To hear me? Let me go: take back thy gift:
Why should a man desire in any way
To vary from the kindly race of men,
Or pass beyond the goal of ordinance
Where all should pause, as is most meet for all?

A soft air fans the cloud apart; there comes
A glimpse of that dark world where I was born.
Once more the old mysterious glimmer steals
From thy pure brows, and from thy shoulders pure,
And bosom beating with a heart renew'd.
Thy cheek begins to redden thro' the gloom,
Thy sweet eyes brighten slowly close to mine,
Ere yet they blind the stars, and the wild team
Which love thee, yearning for thy yoke, arise,
And shake the darkness from their loosen'd manes,
And beat the twilight into flakes of fire.

Lo! ever thus thou growest beautiful
In silence, then before thine answer given
Departest, and thy tears are on my cheek.

  Why wilt thou ever scare me with thy tears,
And make me tremble lest a saying learnt,
In days far-off, on that dark earth, be true?
'The Gods themselves cannot recall their gifts.'

  Ay me! ay me! with what another heart
In days far-off, and with what other eyes
I used to watch—if I be he that watch'd—
The lucid outline forming round thee; saw
The dim curls kindle into sunny rings;
Changed with thy mystic change, and felt my blood
Glow with the glow that slowly crimson'd all
Thy presence and thy portals, while I lay,
Mouth, forehead, eyelids, growing dewy-warm
With kisses balmier than half-opening buds
Of April, and could hear the lips that kiss'd
Whispering I knew not what of wild and sweet,
Like that strange song I heard Apollo sing,
While Ilion like a mist rose into towers.

  Yet hold me not for ever in thine East:
How can my nature longer mix with thine?
Coldly thy rosy shadows bathe me, cold
Are all thy lights, and cold my wrinkled feet
Upon thy glimmering thresholds, when the steam
Floats up from those dim fields about the homes
Of happy men that have the power to die,
And grassy barrows of the happier dead.
Release me, and restore me to the ground;

Thou seëst all things, thou wilt see my grave;
Thou wilt renew thy beauty morn by morn;
I earth in earth forget these empty courts,
And thee returning on thy silver wheels.

GODIVA

* * *

AND she, that knew not, pass'd: and all at once,
    With twelve great shocks of sound, the shameless noon
    Was clash'd and hammer'd from a hundred towers,
One after one.

* * *

SIR LAUNCELOT AND QUEEN GUINEVERE

A FRAGMENT

LIKE souls that balance joy and pain,
    With tears and smiles from heaven again
    The maiden Spring upon the plain
Came in a sun-lit fall of rain.
    In crystal vapour everywhere
Blue isles of heaven laugh'd between,
And far, in forest-deeps unseen,
The topmost elm-tree gather'd green
    From draughts of balmy air.

Sometimes the linnet piped his song:
Sometimes the throstle whistled strong:
Sometimes the sparhawk, wheel'd along,
Hush'd all the groves from fear of wrong:

By grassy capes with fuller sound
In curves the yellowing river ran,
And drooping chestnut-buds began
To spread into the perfect fan,
    Above the teeming ground.

Then, in the boyhood of the year,
Sir Launcelot and Queen Guinevere
Rode thro' the coverts of the deer,
With blissful treble ringing clear.
    She seem'd a part of joyous Spring
A gown of grass-green silk she wore,
Buckled with golden clasps before;
A light-green tuft of plumes she bore
    Closed in a golden ring.

Now on some twisted ivy-net,
Now by some tinkling rivulet,
In mosses mixt with violet
Her cream-white mule his pastern set:
    And fleeter now she skimm'd the plains
Than she whose elfin prancer springs
By night to eery warblings,
When all the glimmering moorland rings
    With jingling bridle-reins.

As fast she fled thro' sun and shade,
The happy winds upon her play'd,
Blowing the ringlet from the braid:
She look'd so lovely, as she sway'd
    The rein with dainty finger-tips,

A man had given all other bliss,
And all his worldly worth for this,
To waste his whole heart in one kiss
    Upon her perfect lips.

A FAREWELL

Flow down, cold rivulet, to the sea,
    Thy tribute wave deliver:
No more by thee my steps shall be,
    For ever and for ever.

Flow, softly flow, by lawn and lea,
    A rivulet then a river:
Nowhere by thee my steps shall be,
    For ever and for ever.

But here will sigh thine alder tree,
    And here thine aspen shiver;
And here by thee will hum the bee,
    For ever and for ever.

A thousand suns will stream on thee,
    A thousand moons will quiver;
But not by thee my steps shall be,
    For ever and for ever.

THE EAGLE

FRAGMENT

He clasps the crag with crooked hands;
Close to the sun in lonely lands,
Ring'd with the azure world, he stands.

The wrinkled sea beneath him crawls;
He watches from his mountain walls,
And like a thunderbolt he falls.

'COME NOT, WHEN I AM DEAD'

COME not, when I am dead,
    To drop thy foolish tears upon my grave,
To trample round my fallen head,
    And vex the unhappy dust thou wouldst not save.
There let the wind sweep and the plover cry;
    But thou, go by.

Child, if it were thine error or thy crime
    I care no longer, being all unblest:
Wed whom thou wilt, but I am sick of Time,
    And I desire to rest.
Pass on, weak heart, and leave me where I lie:
    Go by, go by.

THE VISION OF SIN

I

I HAD a vision when the night was late:
A youth came riding toward a palace-gate.
He rode a horse with wings, that would have flown,
But that his heavy rider kept him down.
And from the palace came a child of sin,
And took him by the curls, and led him in,
Where sat a company with heated eyes,
Expecting when a fountain should arise:

A sleepy light upon their brows and lips—
As when the sun, a crescent of eclipse,
Dreams over lake and lawn, and isles and capes—
Suffused them, sitting, lying, languid shapes,
By heaps of gourds, and skins of wine, and piles of grapes.

II

Then methought I heard a mellow sound,
Gathering up from all the lower ground;
Narrowing in to where they sat assembled
Low voluptuous music winding trembled,
Wov'n in circles: they that heard it sigh'd,
Panted hand-in-hand with faces pale,
Swung themselves, and in low tones replied;
Till the fountain spouted, showering wide
Sleet of diamond-drift and pearly hail;
Then the music touch'd the gates and died;
Rose again from where it seem'd to fail,
Storm'd in orbs of song, a growing gale;
Till thronging in and in, to where they waited,
As 'twere a hundred-throated nightingale,
The strong tempestuous treble throbb'd and palpitated;
Ran into its giddiest whirl of sound,
Caught the sparkles, and in circles,
Purple gauzes, golden hazes, liquid mazes,
Flung the torrent rainbow round:
Then they started from their places,
Moved with violence, changed in hue,
Caught each other with wild grimaces,
Half-invisible to the view,
Wheeling with precipitate paces
To the melody, till they flew,

Hair, and eyes, and limbs, and faces,
Twisted hard in fierce embraces,
Like to Furies, like to Graces,
Dash'd together in blinding dew:
Till, kill'd with some luxurious agony,
The nerve-dissolving melody
Flutter'd headlong from the sky.

III

And then I look'd up toward a mountain-tract,
That girt the region with high cliff and lawn:
I saw that every morning, far withdrawn
Beyond the darkness and the cataract,
God made Himself an awful rose of dawn,
Unheeded: and detaching, fold by fold,
From those still heights, and, slowly drawing near,
A vapour heavy, hueless, formless, cold,
Came floating on for many a month and year,
Unheeded: and I thought I would have spoken,
And warn'd that madman ere it grew too late:
But, as in dreams, I could not. Mine was broken,
When that cold vapour touch'd the palace gate,
And link'd again. I saw within my head
A gray and gap-tooth'd man as lean as death,
Who slowly rode across a wither'd heath,
And lighted at a ruin'd inn, and said:

IV

'Wrinkled ostler, grim and thin!
　　Here is custom come your way;
Take my brute, and lead him in,
　　Stuff his ribs with mouldy hay.

'Bitter barmaid, waning fast!
　See that sheets are on my bed;
What! the flower of life is past:
　It is long before you wed.

'Slip-shod waiter, lank and sour,
　At the Dragon on the heath!
Let us have a quiet hour,
　Let us hob-and-nob with Death.

'I am old, but let me drink;
　Bring me spices, bring me wine;
I remember, when I think,
　That my youth was half divine.

'Wine is good for shrivell'd lips,
　When a blanket wraps the day,
When the rotten woodland drips,
　And the leaf is stamp'd in clay.

'Sit thee down, and have no shame,
　Cheek by jowl, and knee by knee:
What care I for any name?
　What for order or degree?

'Let me screw thee up a peg:
　Let me loose thy tongue with wine:
Callest thou that thing a leg?
　Which is thinnest? thine or mine?

'Thou shalt not be saved by works:
　Thou hast been a sinner too:
Ruin'd trunks on wither'd forks,
　Empty scarecrows, I and you!

'Fill the cup, and fill the can:
   Have a rouse before the morn:
Every moment dies a man,
   Every moment one is born.

'We are men of ruin'd blood;
   Therefore comes it we are wise.
Fish are we that love the mud,
   Rising to no fancy-flies.

'Name and fame! to fly sublime
   Thro' the courts, the camps, the schools,
Is to be the ball of Time,
   Bandied by the hands of fools.

'Friendship!—to be two in one—
   Let the canting liar pack!
Well I know, when I am gone,
   How she mouths behind my back.

'Virtue!—to be good and just—
   Every heart, when sifted well,
Is a clot of warmer dust,
   Mix'd with cunning sparks of hell.

'O! we two as well can look
   Whited thought and cleanly life
As the priest, above his book
   Leering at his neighbour's wife.

'Fill the cup, and fill the can:
   Have a rouse before the morn:
Every moment dies a man,
   Every moment one is born.

'Drink, and let the parties rave:
   They are fill'd with idle spleen;
Rising, falling, like a wave,
   For they know not what they mean.

'He that roars for liberty
   Faster binds a tyrant's power;
And the tyrant's cruel glee
   Forces on the freer hour.

'Fill the can, and fill the cup:
   All the windy ways of men
Are but dust that rises up,
   And is lightly laid again.

'Greet her with applausive breath,
   Freedom, gaily doth she tread;
In her right a civic wreath,
   In her left a human head.

'No, I love not what is new;
   She is of an ancient house:
And I think we know the hue
   Of that cap upon her brows.

'Let her go! her thirst she slakes
   Where the bloody conduit runs,
Then her sweetest meal she makes
   On the first-born of her sons.

'Drink to lofty hopes that cool—
   Visions of a perfect State:
Drink we, last, the public fool,
   Frantic love and frantic hate.

'Chant me now some wicked stave,
   Till thy drooping courage rise,
And the glow-worm of the grave
   Glimmer in thy rheumy eyes.

'Fear not thou to loose thy tongue;
   Set thy hoary fancies free;
What is loathsome to the young
   Savours well to thee and me.

'Change, reverting to the years,
   When thy nerves could understand
What there is in loving tears,
   And the warmth of hand in hand.

'Tell me tales of thy first love—
   April hopes, the fools of chance;
Till the graves begin to move,
   And the dead begin to dance.

'Fill the can, and fill the cup:
   All the windy ways of men
Are but dust that rises up,
   And is lightly laid again.

'Trooping from their mouldy dens
   The chap-fallen circle spreads:
Welcome, fellow-citizens,
   Hollow hearts and empty heads!

'You are bones, and what of that?
   Every face, however full,
Padded round with flesh and fat,
   Is but modell'd on a skull.

'Death is king, and Vivat Rex!
   Tread a measure on the stones,
Madam—if I know your sex,
   From the fashion of your bones.

'No, I cannot praise the fire
   In your eye—nor yet your lip:
All the more do I admire
   Joints of cunning workmanship.

'Lo! God's likeness—the ground-plan—
   Neither modell'd, glazed, nor framed:
Buss me, thou rough sketch of man,
   Far too naked to be shamed!

'Drink to Fortune, drink to Chance,
   While we keep a little breath!
Drink to heavy Ignorance!
   Hob-and-nob with brother Death!

'Thou art mazed, the night is long,
   And the longer night is near:
What! I am not all as wrong
   As a bitter jest is dear.

'Youthful hopes, by scores, to all,
   When the locks are crisp and curl'd;
Unto me my maudlin gall
   And my mockeries of the world.

'Fill the cup, and fill the can:
   Mingle madness, mingle scorn!
Dregs of life, and lees of man:
   Yet we will not die forlorn'.

V

The voice grew faint: there came a further change:
Once more uprose the mystic mountain-range:
Below were men and horses pierced with worms,
And slowly quickening into lower forms;
By shards and scurf of salt, and scum of dross,
Old plash of rains, and refuse patch'd with moss.
Then some one spake: 'Behold! it was a crime
Of sense avenged by sense that wore with time'.
Another said: 'The crime of sense became
The crime of malice, and is equal blame'.
And one: 'He had not wholly quench'd his power;
A little grain of conscience made him sour'.
At last I heard a voice upon the slope
Cry to the summit, 'Is there any hope?'
To which an answer peal'd from that high land,
But in a tongue no man could understand;
And on the glimmering limit far withdrawn
God made Himself an awful rose of dawn.

TO E. L., ON HIS TRAVELS IN GREECE

ILLYRIAN woodlands, echoing falls
   Of water, sheets of summer glass,
   The long divine Peneïan pass,
The vast Akrokeraunian walls,

Tomohrit, Athos, all things fair,
   With such a pencil, such a pen,
   You shadow forth to distant men,
I read and felt that I was there:

And trust me while I turn'd the page,
   And track'd you still on classic ground,
   I grew in gladness till I found
My spirits in the golden age.

For me the torrent ever pour'd
   And glisten'd—here and there alone
   The broad-limb'd Gods at random thrown
By fountain-urns;—and Naiads oar'd

A glimmering shoulder under gloom
   Of cavern pillars; on the swell
   The silver lily heaved and fell;
And many a slope was rich in bloom

From him that on the mountain lea
   By dancing rivulets fed his flocks
   To him who sat upon the rocks,
And fluted to the morning sea.

'BREAK, BREAK, BREAK...'

BREAK, break, break,
   On thy cold gray stones, O Sea!
And I would that my tongue could utter
   The thoughts that arise in me.

O well for the fisherman's boy,
   That he shouts with his sister at play!
O well for the sailor lad,
   That he sings in his boat on the bay!

And the stately ships go on
    To their haven under the hill;
But O for the touch of a vanish'd hand,
    And the sound of a voice that is still!

Break, break, break,
    At the foot of thy crags, O Sea!
But the tender grace of a day that is dead
    Will never come back to me.

THE PRINCESS; A MEDLEY

*   *   *

'Tears, idle tears, I know not what they mean,
    Tears from the depth of some divine despair
    Rise in the heart, and gather to the eyes,
In looking on the happy Autumn-fields,
And thinking of the days that are no more.

'Fresh as the first beam glittering on a sail,
That brings our friends up from the underworld,
Sad as the last which reddens over one
That sinks with all we love below the verge;
So sad, so fresh, the days that are no more.

'Ah, sad and strange as in dark summer dawns
The earliest pipe of half-awaken'd birds
To dying ears, when unto dying eyes
The casement slowly grows a glimmering square;
So sad, so strange, the days that are no more.

'Dear as remember'd kisses after death,
And sweet as those by hopeless fancy feign'd
On lips that are for others; deep as love,
Deep as first love, and wild with all regret;
O Death in Life, the days that are no more.'

* * *

Ask me no more: the moon may draw the sea;
  The cloud may stoop from heaven and take the shape
  With fold to fold, of mountain or of cape;
But O too fond, when have I answer'd thee?
               Ask me no more.

Ask me no more: what answer should I give?
  I love not hollow cheek or faded eye:
  Yet, O my friend, I will not have thee die!
Ask me no more, lest I should bid thee live;
               Ask me no more.

Ask me no more: thy fate and mine are seal'd:
  I strove against the stream and all in vain:
  Let the great river take me to the main:
No more, dear love, for at a touch I yield;
               Ask me no more.

* * *

And she as one that climbs a peak to gaze
O'er land and main, and sees a great black cloud
Drag inward from the deeps, a wall of night,
Blot out the slope of sea from verge to shore,
And suck the blinding splendour from the sand,
And quenching lake by lake and tarn by tarn
Expunge the world: so fared she gazing there;

So blacken'd all her world in secret, blank
And waste it seem'd and vain; till down she came,
And found fair peace once more among the sick.

   And twilight dawn'd; and morn by morn the lark
Shot up and shrill'd in flickering gyres, but I
Lay silent in the muffled cage of life:
And twilight gloom'd; and broader-grown the bowers
Drew the great night into themselves, and Heaven,
Star after star, arose and fell; but I,
Deeper than those weird doubts could reach me, lay
Quite sunder'd from the moving Universe,
Nor knew what eye was on me, nor the hand
That nursed me, more than infants in their sleep.

        *   *   *

And watches in the dead, the dark, when clocks
Throbb'd thunder thro' the palace floors, or call'd
On flying Time from all their silver tongues—

        *   *   *

   'Now sleeps the crimson petal, now the white;
Nor waves the cypress in the palace walk;
Nor winks the gold fin in the porphyry font:
The fire-fly wakens: waken thou with me.

   Now droops the milkwhite peacock like a ghost,
And like a ghost she glimmers on to me.

   Now lies the Earth all Danaë to the stars,
And all thy heart lies open unto me.

   Now slides the silent meteor on, and leaves
A shining furrow, as thy thoughts in me.

Now folds the lily all her sweetness up,
And slips into the bosom of the lake:
So fold thyself, my dearest, thou, and slip
Into my bosom and be lost in me.'

*　　　*　　　*

'Come down, O maid, from yonder mountain height:
What pleasure lives in height (the shepherd sang)
In height and cold, the splendour of the hills?
But cease to move so near the Heavens, and cease
To glide a sunbeam by the blasted Pine,
To sit a star upon the sparkling spire;
And come, for Love is of the valley, come,
For Love is of the valley, come thou down
And find him; by the happy threshold, he,
Or hand in hand with Plenty in the maize,
Or red with spirted purple of the vats,
Or foxlike in the vine; nor cares to walk
With Death and Morning on the silver horns,
Nor wilt thou snare him in the white ravine,
Nor find him dropt upon the firths of ice,
That huddling slant in furrow-cloven falls
To roll the torrent out of dusky doors:
But follow; let the torrent dance thee down
To find him in the valley; let the wild
Lean-headed Eagles yelp alone, and leave
The monstrous ledges there to slope, and spill
Their thousand wreaths of dangling water-smoke,
That like a broken purpose waste in air:
So waste not thou: but come; for all the vales
Await thee; azure pillars of the hearth
Arise to thee; the children call, and I

Thy shepherd pipe, and sweet is every sound,
Sweeter thy voice, but every sound is sweet;
Myriads of rivulets hurrying thro' the lawn,
The moan of doves in immemorial elms,
And murmuring of innumerable bees'.

* * *

In that fine air I tremble, all the past
Melts mist-like into this bright hour, and this
Is morn to more, and all the rich to-come
Reels, as the golden Autumn woodland reels
Athwart the smoke of burning weeds.

* * *

              We climb'd
The slope to Vivian-place, and turning saw
The happy valleys, half in light, and half
Far-shadowing from the west, a land of peace;
Gray halls alone among their massive groves;
Trim hamlets; here and there a rustic tower
Half-lost in belts of hop and breadths of wheat;
The shimmering glimpses of a stream; the seas;
A red sail, or a white; and far beyond,
Imagined more than seen, the skirts of France.

* * *

IN MEMORIAM A. H. H.
OBIIT MDCCCXXXIII

II

OLD Yew, which graspest at the stones
    That name the under-lying dead,
    Thy fibres net the dreamless head,
Thy roots are wrapt about the bones.

The seasons bring the flower again,
    And bring the firstling to the flock;
    And in the dusk of thee, the clock
Beats out the little lives of men.
O not for thee the glow, the bloom,
    Who changest not in any gale,
    Nor branding summer suns avail
To touch thy thousand years of gloom:
And gazing on thee, sullen tree,
    Sick for thy stubborn hardihood,
    I seem to fail from out my blood
And grow incorporate into thee.

III

O Sorrow, cruel fellowship,
    O Priestess in the vaults of Death,
    O sweet and bitter in a breath,
What whispers from thy lying lip?
'The stars', she whispers, 'blindly run;
    A web is wov'n across the sky;
    From out waste places comes a cry,
And murmurs from the dying sun:
'And all the phantom, Nature, stands—
    With all the music in her tone,
    A hollow echo of my own,—
A hollow form with empty hands.'

*   *   *

VII

Dark house, by which once more I stand
    Here in the long unlovely street,
    Doors, where my heart was used to beat
So quickly, waiting for a hand,

A hand that can be clasp'd no more—
    Behold me, for I cannot sleep,
    And like a guilty thing I creep
At earliest morning to the door.

He is not here; but far away
    The noise of life begins again,
    And ghastly thro' the drizzling rain
On the bald street breaks the blank day.

XI

Calm is the morn without a sound,
    Calm as to suit a calmer grief,
    And only thro' the faded leaf
The chestnut pattering to the ground:

Calm and deep peace on this high wold,
    And on these dews that drench the furze,
    And all the silvery gossamers
That twinkle into green and gold:

Calm and still light on yon great plain
    That sweeps with all its autumn bowers.
    And crowded farms and lessening towers,
To mingle with the bounding main:

Calm and deep peace in this wide air,
    These leaves that redden to the fall;
    And in my heart, if calm at all,
If any calm, a calm despair:

Calm on the seas, and silver sleep,
    And waves that sway themselves in rest,
    And dead calm in that noble breast
Which heaves but with the heaving deep.

XV

To-night the winds begin to rise
    And roar from yonder dropping day:
    The last red leaf is whirl'd away,
The rooks are blown about the skies;

The forest crack'd, the waters curl'd,
    The cattle huddled on the lea;
    And wildly dash'd on tower and tree
The sunbeam strikes along the world:

And but for fancies, which aver
    That all thy motions gently pass
    Athwart a plane of molten glass,
I scarce could brook the strain and stir

That makes the barren branches loud;
    And but for fear it is not so,
    The wild unrest that lives in woe
Would dote and pore on yonder cloud

That rises upward always higher,
    And onward drags a labouring breast,
    And topples round the dreary west,
A looming bastion fringed with fire.

XIX

The Danube to the Severn gave
    The darken'd heart that beat no more;
    They laid him by the pleasant shore,
And in the hearing of the wave.

There twice a day the Severn fills;
    The salt sea-water passes by,
    And hushes half the babbling Wye,
And makes a silence in the hills.

The Wye is hush'd nor moved along,
    And hush'd my deepest grief of all,
    When fill'd with tears that cannot fall,
I brim with sorrow drowning song.

The tide flows down, the wave again
    Is vocal in its wooded walls;
    My deeper anguish also falls,
And I can speak a little then.

XXI

I sing to him that rests below,
    And, since the grasses round me wave,
    I take the grasses of the grave,
And make them pipes whereon to blow.

The traveller hears me now and then,
    And sometimes harshly will he speak:
    'This fellow would make weakness weak,
And melt the waxen hearts of men'.

Another answers, 'Let him be,
    He loves to make parade of pain,
    That with his piping he may gain
The praise that comes to constancy'.

A third is wroth: 'Is this an hour
    For private sorrow's barren song,
    When more and more the people throng
The chairs and thrones of civil power?

'A time to sicken and to swoon,
    When Science reaches forth her arms
    To feel from world to world, and charms
Her secret from the latest moon?'

Behold, ye speak an idle thing:
> Ye never knew the sacred dust:
> I do but sing because I must,
And pipe but as the linnets sing:

And one is glad; her note is gay,
> For now her little ones have ranged;
> And one is sad; her note is changed,
Because her brood is stol'n away.

XXIII

Now, sometimes in my sorrow shut,
> Or breaking into song by fits,
> Alone, alone, to where he sits,
The Shadow cloak'd from head to foot,

Who keeps the keys of all the creeds,
> I wander, often falling lame,
> And looking back to whence I came,
Or on to where the pathway leads;

And crying, How changed from where it ran
> Thro' lands where not a leaf was dumb;
> But all the lavish hills would hum
The murmur of a happy Pan:

When each by turns was guide to each,
> And Fancy light from Fancy caught,
> And Thought leapt out to wed with Thought
Ere Thought could wed itself with Speech;

And all we met was fair and good,
> And all was good that Time could bring,
> And all the secret of the Spring
Moved in the chambers of the blood;

And many an old philosophy
    On Argive heights divinely sang,
    And round us all the thicket rang
To many a flute of Arcady.

XXVI

Still onward winds the dreary way;
    I with it; for I long to prove
    No lapse of moons can canker Love,
Whatever fickle tongues may say.

And if that eye which watches guilt
    And goodness, and hath power to see
    Within the green the moulder'd tree,
And towers fall'n as soon as built—

Oh, if indeed that eye foresee
    Or see (in Him is no before)
    In more of life true life no more
And Love the indifference to be,

Then might I find, ere yet the morn
    Breaks hither over Indian seas,
    That Shadow waiting with the keys,
To shroud me from my proper scorn.

XXXI

When Lazarus left his charnel-cave,
    And home to Mary's house return'd,
    Was this demanded—if he yearn'd
To hear her weeping by his grave?

'Where wert thou, brother, those four days?'
    There lives no record of reply,
    Which telling what it is to die
Had surely added praise to praise.

From every house the neighbours met,
    The streets were fill'd with joyful sound,
    A solemn gladness even crown'd
The purple brows of Olivet.

Behold a man raised up by Christ!
    The rest remaineth unreveal'd;
    He told it not; or something seal'd
The lips of that Evangelist.

XXXIV

My own dim life should teach me this,
    That life shall live for evermore,
    Else earth is darkness at the core,
And dust and ashes all that is;

This round of green, this orb of flame,
    Fantastic beauty; such as lurks
    In some wild Poet, when he works
Without a conscience or an aim.

What then were God to such as I?
    'Twere hardly worth my while to choose
    Of things all mortal, or to use
A little patience ere I die;

'Twere best at once to sink to peace,
    Like birds the charming serpent draws,
    To drop head-foremost in the jaws
Of vacant darkness and to cease.

XXXV

Yet if some voice that man could trust
    Should murmur from the narrow house,
    'The cheeks drop in; the body bows;
Man dies: nor is there hope in dust':

Might I not say? 'Yet even here,
    But for one hour, O Love, I strive
    To keep so sweet a thing alive':
But I should turn mine ears and hear

The moanings of the homeless sea,
    The sound of streams that swift or slow
    Draw down Æonian hills, and sow
The dust of continents to be;

And Love would answer with a sigh,
    'The sound of that forgetful shore
    Will change my sweetness more and more,
Half-dead to know that I shall die'.

O me, what profits it to put
    An idle case? If Death were seen
    At first as Death, Love had not been,
Or been in narrowest working shut,

Mere fellowship of sluggish moods,
    Or in his coarsest Satyr-shape
    Had bruised the herb and crush'd the grape,
And bask'd and batten'd in the woods.

XXXIX

Old warder of these buried bones,
    And answering now my random stroke
    With fruitful cloud and living smoke,
Dark yew, that graspest at the stones

And dippest toward the dreamless head,
    To thee too comes the golden hour
    When flower is feeling after flower;
But Sorrow—fixt upon the dead,

And darkening the dark graves of men,—
    What whisper'd from her lying lips?
    Thy gloom is kindled at the tips,
And passes into gloom again.

L

Be near me when my light is low,
    When the blood creeps, and the nerves prick
    And tingle; and the heart is sick,
And all the wheels of Being slow.

Be near me when the sensuous frame
    Is rack'd with pangs that conquer trust;
    And Time, a maniac scattering dust,
And Life, a Fury slinging flame.

Be near me when my faith is dry,
    And men the flies of latter spring,
    That lay their eggs, and sting and sing
And weave their petty cells and die.

Be near me when I fade away,
    To point the term of human strife,
    And on the low dark verge of life
The twilight of eternal day.

LIV

Oh yet we trust that somehow good
    Will be the final goal of ill,
    To pangs of nature, sins of will,
Defects of doubt, and taints of blood;

That nothing walks with aimless feet;
    That not one life shall be destroy'd,
    Or cast as rubbish to the void,
When God hath made the pile complete;

That not a worm is cloven in vain;
    That not a moth with vain desire
    Is shrivell'd in a fruitless fire,
Or but subserves another's gain.

Behold, we know not anything;
    I can but trust that good shall fall
    At last—far off—at last, to all,
And every winter change to spring.

So runs my dream: but what am I?
    An infant crying in the night:
    An infant crying for the light:
And with no language but a cry.

LVI

'So careful of the type?' but no.
    From scarped cliff and quarried stone
    She cries, 'A thousand types are gone:
I care for nothing, all shall go.

'Thou makest thine appeal to me:
    I bring to life, I bring to death:
    The spirit does but mean the breath:
I know no more'. And he, shall he,

Man, her last work, who seem'd so fair,
    Such splendid purpose in his eyes,
    Who roll'd the psalm to wintry skies,
Who built him fanes of fruitless prayer,

Who trusted God was love indeed
    And love Creation's final law—
    Tho' Nature, red in tooth and claw
With ravine, shriek'd against his creed—

Who loved, who suffer'd countless ills,
    Who battled for the True, the Just,
    Be blown about the desert dust,
Or seal'd within the iron hills?

No more? A monster then, a dream,
    A discord. Dragons of the prime,
    That tare each other in their slime,
Were mellow music match'd with him.

O life as futile, then, as frail!
    O for thy voice to soothe and bless!
    What hope of answer, or redress?
Behind the veil, behind the veil.

LXIV

Dost thou look back on what hath been,
    As some divinely gifted man,
    Whose life in low estate began
And on a simple village green;

Who breaks his birth's invidious bar,
    And grasps the skirts of happy chance,
    And breasts the blows of circumstance,
And grapples with his evil star;

Who makes by force his merit known
    And lives to clutch the golden keys,
    To mould a mighty state's decrees,
And shape the whisper of the throne;

And moving up from high to higher,
    Becomes on Fortune's crowning slope
    The pillar of a people's hope,
The centre of a world's desire;

Yet feels, as in a pensive dream,
    When all his active powers are still,
    A distant dearness in the hill,
A secret sweetness in the stream,

The limit of his narrower fate,
    While yet beside its vocal springs
    He play'd at counsellors and kings,
With one that was his earliest mate;

Who ploughs with pain his native lea
    And reaps the labour of his hands,
    Or in the furrow musing stands;
'Does my old friend remember me?'

LXVII

When on my bed the moonlight falls,
    I know that in thy place of rest
    By that broad water of the west,
There comes a glory on the walls:

Thy marble bright in dark appears,
    As slowly steals a silver flame
    Along the letters of thy name,
And o'er the number of thy years.

The mystic glory swims away;
    From off my bed the moonlight dies;
    And closing eaves of wearied eyes
I sleep till dusk is dipt in gray:

And then I know the mist is drawn
    A lucid veil from coast to coast,
    And in the dark church like a ghost
Thy tablet glimmers to the dawn.

LXXII

Risest thou thus, dim dawn, again,
    And howlest, issuing out of night,
    With blasts that blow the poplar white,
And lash with storm the streaming pane?

Day, when my crown'd estate begun
    To pine in that reverse of doom,
    Which sicken'd every living bloom,
And blurr'd the splendour of the sun;

Who usherest in the dolorous hour
    With thy quick tears that make the rose
    Pull sideways, and the daisy close
Her crimson fringes to the shower;

Who might'st have heaved a windless flame
    Up the deep East, or, whispering, play'd
    A chequer-work of beam and shade
Along the hills, yet look'd the same.

As wan, as chill, as wild as now;
    Day, mark'd as with some hideous crime,
    When the dark hand struck down thro' time,
And cancell'd nature's best: but thou,

Lift as thou may'st thy burthen'd brows
    Thro' clouds that drench the morning star,
    And whirl the ungarner'd sheaf afar,
And sow the sky with flying boughs,

And up thy vault with roaring sound
    Climb thy thick noon, disastrous day;
    Touch thy dull goal of joyless gray,
And hide thy shame beneath the ground.

LXXIV

As sometimes in a dead man's face,
    To those that watch it more and more,
    A likeness, hardly seen before,
Comes out—to some one of his race:

So, dearest, now thy brows are cold,
    I see thee what thou art, and know
    Thy likeness to the wise below,
Thy kindred with the great of old.

But there is more than I can see,
    And what I see I leave unsaid,
    Nor speak it, knowing Death has made
His darkness beautiful with thee.

LXXVI

Take wings of fancy, and ascend,
    And in a moment set thy face
    Where all the starry heavens of space
Are sharpen'd to a needle's end;

Take wings of foresight; lighten thro'
    The secular abyss to come,
    And lo, thy deepest lays are dumb
Before the mouldering of a yew;

And if the matin songs, that woke
    The darkness of our planet, last,
    Thine own shall wither in the vast,
Ere half the lifetime of an oak.

Ere these have clothed their branchy bowers
    With fifty Mays, thy songs are vain;
    And what are they when these remain
The ruin'd shells of hollow towers?

XCV

*   *   *

Till now the doubtful dusk reveal'd
    The knolls once more where, couch'd at ease,
    The white kine glimmer'd, and the trees
Laid their dark arms about the field:

And suck'd from out the distant gloom
    A breeze began to tremble o'er
    The large leaves of the sycamore,
And fluctuate all the still perfume,

And gathering freshlier overhead,
    Rock'd the full-foliaged elms, and swung
    The heavy-folded rose, and flung
The lilies to and fro, and said

'The dawn, the dawn', and died away;
    And East and West, without a breath,
    Mixt their dim lights, like life and death,
To broaden into boundless day.

CI

Unwatch'd, the garden bough shall sway,
    The tender blossom flutter down,
    Unloved, that beech will gather brown,
This maple burn itself away;

Unloved, the sun-flower, shining fair,
> Ray round with flames her disk of seed,
> And many a rose-carnation feed
With summer spice the humming air;

Unloved, by many a sandy bar,
> The brook shall babble down the plain,
> At noon or when the lesser wain
Is twisting round the polar star;

Uncared for, gird the windy grove,
> And flood the haunts of hern and crake;
> Or into silver arrows break
The sailing moon in creek and cove;

Till from the garden and the wild
> A fresh association blow,
> And year by year the landscape grow
Familiar to the stranger's child;

As year by year the labourer tills
> His wonted glebe, or lops the glades;
> And year by year our memory fades
From all the circle of the hills.

CVII

It is the day when he was born,
> A bitter day that early sank
> Behind a purple-frosty bank
Of vapour, leaving night forlorn.

The time admits not flowers or leaves
> To deck the banquet. Fiercely flies
> The blast of North and East, and ice
Makes daggers at the sharpen'd eaves,

And bristles all the brakes and thorns
>   To yon hard crescent, as she hangs
>   Above the wood which grides and clangs
Its leafless ribs and iron horns

Together, in the drifts that pass
>   To darken on the rolling brine
>   That breaks the coast. But fetch the wine,
Arrange the board and brim the glass;

Bring in great logs and let them lie,
>   To make a solid core of heat;
>   Be cheerful-minded, talk and treat
Of all things ev'n as he were by;

We keep the day. With festal cheer,
>   With books and music, surely we
>   Will drink to him, whate'er he be,
And sing the songs he loved to hear.

CXV

Now fades the last long streak of snow,
>   Now burgeons every maze of quick
>   About the flowering squares, and thick
By ashen roots the violets blow.

Now rings the woodland loud and long,
>   The distance takes a lovelier hue,
>   And drown'd in yonder living blue
The lark becomes a sightless song.

Now dance the lights on lawn and lea,
>   The flocks are whiter down the vale,
>   And milkier every milky sail
On winding stream or distant sea;

Where now the seamew pipes, or dives
    In yonder greening gleam, and fly
    The happy birds, that change their sky
To build and brood; that live their lives

From land to land; and in my breast
    Spring wakens too; and my regret
    Becomes an April violet,
And buds and blossoms like the rest.

CXXIII

There rolls the deep where grew the tree.
    O earth, what changes hast thou seen!
    There where the long street roars, hath been
The stillness of the central sea.

The hills are shadows, and they flow
    From form to form, and nothing stands;
    They melt like mist, the solid lands,
Like clouds they shape themselves and go.

But in my spirit will I dwell,
    And dream my dream, and hold it true;
    For tho' my lips may breathe adieu,
I cannot think the thing farewell.

CXXIV

That which we dare invoke to bless;
    Our dearest faith; our ghastliest doubt;
    He, They, One, All; within, without;
The Power in darkness whom we guess;

I found Him not in world or sun,
    Or eagle's wing, or insect's eye;
    Nor thro' the questions men may try,
The petty cobwebs we have spun:

If e'er when faith had fall'n asleep,
    I heard a voice 'believe no more'
    And heard an ever-breaking shore
That tumbled in the Godless deep;

A warmth within the breast would melt
    The freezing reason's colder part,
    And like a man in wrath the heart
Stood up and answer'd 'I have felt'.

No, like a child in doubt and fear:
    But that blind clamour made me wise
    Then was I as a child that cries,
But, crying, knows his father near;

And what I am beheld again
    What is, and no man understands;
    And out of darkness came the hands
That reach thro' nature, moulding men.

CXXXI

*   *   *

And rise, O moon, from yonder down,
    Till over down and over dale
    All night the shining vapour sail
And pass the silent-lighted town,

The white-faced halls, the glancing rills,
    And catch at every mountain head,
    And o'er the friths that branch and spread
Their sleeping silver thro' the hills.

*   *   *

MAUD; A MONODRAMA
PART I III

* * *

     Till I could bear it no more,
But arose, and all by myself in my own dark garden ground,
Listening now to the tide in its broad-flung ship-wrecking roar,
Now to the scream of a madden'd beach dragg'd down by
 the wave,
Walk'd in a wintry wind by a ghastly glimmer, and found
The shining daffodil dead, and Orion low in his grave.

XVII
  Go not, happy day,
    From the shining fields,
  Go not, happy day,
    Till the maiden yields.
  Rosy is the West,
    Rosy is the South,
  Roses are her cheeks,
    And a rose her mouth.
  When the happy Yes
    Falters from her lips,
  Pass and blush the news
    Over glowing ships;
  Over blowing seas,
    Over seas at rest,
  Pass the happy news,
    Blush it thro' the West;
  Till the red man dance
    By his red cedar-tree,
  And the red man's babe
    Leap, beyond the sea.

Blush from West to East,
   Blush from East to West,
Till the West is East,
   Blush it thro' the West.
Rosy is the West,
   Rosy is the South,
Roses are her cheeks,
   And a rose her mouth.

XXII

I

Come into the garden, Maud,
   For the black bat, night, has flown,
Come into the garden, Maud,
   I am here at the gate alone;
And the woodbine spices are wafted abroad,
   And the musk of the rose is blown.

II

For a breeze of morning moves,
   And the planet of Love is on high,
Beginning to faint in the light that she loves
   On a bed of daffodil sky,
To faint in the light of the sun she loves,
   To faint in his light, and to die.

III

All night have the roses heard
   The flute, violin, bassoon;
All night has the casement jessamine stirr'd
   To the dancers dancing in tune;
Till a silence fell with the waking bird,
   And a hush with the setting moon.

IV

I said to the lily, 'There is but one
   With whom she has heart to be gay.
When will the dancers leave her alone?
   She is weary of dance and play'.
Now half to the setting moon are gone,
   And half to the rising day;
Low on the sand and loud on the stone
   The last wheel echoes away.

V

I said to the rose, 'The brief night goes
   In babble and revel and wine.
O young lord-lover, what sighs are those,
   For one that will never be thine?
But mine, but mine', so I sware to the rose,
   'For ever and ever, mine'.

VI

And the soul of the rose went into my blood,
   As the music clash'd in the hall;
And long by the garden lake I stood,
   For I heard your rivulet fall
From the lake to the meadow and on to the wood,
   Our wood, that is dearer than all;

VII

From the meadow your walks have left so sweet
   That whenever a March-wind sighs
He sets the jewel-print of your feet
   In violets blue as your eyes,
To the woody hollows in which we meet
   And the valleys of Paradise.

VIII

The slender acacia would not shake
    One long milk-bloom on the tree;
The white lake-blossom fell into the lake
    As the pimpernel dozed on the lea;
But the rose was awake all night for your sake,
    Knowing your promise to me;
The lilies and roses were all awake,
    They sigh'd for the dawn and thee.

IX

Queen rose of the rosebud garden of girls,
    Come hither, the dances are done,
In gloss of satin and glimmer of pearls,
    Queen lily and rose in one;
Shine out, little head, sunning over with curls,
    To the flowers, and be their sun.

X

There has fallen a splendid tear
    From the passion-flower at the gate.
She is coming, my dove, my dear;
    She is coming, my life, my fate;
The red rose cries, 'She is near, she is near';
    And the white rose weeps, 'She is late';
The larkspur listens, 'I hear, I hear';
    And the lily whispers, 'I wait'.

XI

She is coming, my own, my sweet;
    Were it ever so airy a tread,
My heart would hear her and beat,
    Were it earth in an earthy bed;

My dust would hear her and beat,
   Had I lain for a century dead;
Would start and tremble under her feet,
   And blossom in purple and red.

PART II

IV

I

O that 'twere possible
After long grief and pain
To find the arms of my true love
Round me once again!

II

When I was wont to meet her
In the silent woody places
By the home that gave me birth,
We stood tranced in long embraces
Mixt with kisses sweeter sweeter
Than anything on earth.

III

A shadow flits before me,
Not thou, but like to thee:
Ah Christ, that it were possible
For one short hour to see
The souls we loved, that they might tell us
What and where they be.

THE DAISY

WRITTEN AT EDINBURGH

O LOVE, what hours were thine and mine,
In lands of palm and southern pine;
In lands of palm, of orange-blossom,
Of olive, aloe, and maize and vine.

What Roman strength Turbìa show'd
In ruin, by the mountain road;
How like a gem, beneath, the city
Of little Monaco, basking, glow'd.

How richly down the rocky dell
The torrent vineyard streaming fell
To meet the sun and sunny waters,
That only heaved with a summer swell.

What slender campanili grew
By bays, the peacock's neck in hue;
Where, here and there, on sandy beaches
A milky-bell'd amaryllis blew.

How young Columbus seem'd to rove,
Yet present in his natal grove,
Now watching high on mountain cornice,
And steering, now, from a purple cove,

Now pacing mute by ocean's rim;
Till, in a narrow street and dim,
I stay'd the wheels at Cogoletto,
And drank, and loyally drank to him.

Nor knew we well what pleased us most,
Not the clipt palm of which they boast;
   But distant colour, happy hamlet,
A moulder'd citadel on the coast,

Or tower, or high hill-convent, seen
A light amid its olives green;
   Or olive-hoary cape in ocean;
Or rosy blossom in hot ravine,

Where oleanders flush'd the bed
Of silent torrents, gravel-spread;
   And, crossing, oft we saw the glisten
Of ice, far up on a mountain head.

We loved that hall, tho' white and cold,
Those niched shapes of noble mould,
   A princely people's awful princes,
The grave, severe Genovese of old.

At Florence too what golden hours,
In those long galleries, were ours;
   What drives about the fresh Cascinè,
Or walks in Boboli's ducal bowers.

In bright vignettes, and each complete,
Of tower or duomo, sunny-sweet,
   Or palace, how the city glitter'd,
Thro' cypress avenues, at our feet.

But when we crost the Lombard plain
Remember what a plague of rain;
   Of rain at Reggio, rain at Parma;
At Lodi, rain, Piacenza, rain.

And stern and sad (so rare the smiles
Of sunlight) look'd the Lombard piles;
   Porch-pillars on the lion resting,
And sombre, old, colonnaded aisles.

O Milan, O the chanting quires,
The giant windows' blazon'd fires,
   The height, the space, the gloom, the glory!
A mount of marble, a hundred spires!

I climb'd the roofs at break of day;
Sun-smitten Alps before me lay.
   I stood among the silent statues,
And statued pinnacles, mute as they.

How faintly-flush'd, how phantom-fair,
Was Monte Rosa, hanging there
   A thousand shadowy-pencill'd valleys
And snowy dells in a golden air.

Remember how we came at last
To Como; shower and storm and blast
   Had blown the lake beyond his limit,
And all was flooded; and how we past

From Como, when the light was gray,
And in my head, for half the day,
   The rich Virgilian rustic measure
Of Lari Maxume, all the way,

Like ballad-burthen music, kept,
As on The Lariano crept
   To that fair port below the castle
Of Queen Theodolind, where we slept;

Or hardly slept, but watch'd awake
A cypress in the moonlight shake,
   The moonlight touching o'er a terrace
One tall Agavè above the lake.

What more? we took out last adieu,
And up the snowy Splugen drew,
   But ere we reach'd the highest summit
I pluck'd a daisy, I gave it you.

It told of England then to me,
And now it tells of Italy.
   O love, we two shall go no longer
To lands of summer across the sea;

So dear a life your arms enfold
Whose crying is a cry for gold:
   Yet here to-night in this dark city,
When ill and weary, alone and cold,

I found, tho' crush'd to hard and dry,
This nurseling of another sky
   Still in the little book you lent me,
And where you tenderly laid it by:

And I forgot the clouded Forth,
The gloom that saddens Heaven and Earth,
   The bitter east, the misty summer
And gray metropolis of the North.

Perchance, to lull the throbs of pain,
Perchance, to charm a vacant brain,
   Perchance, to dream you still beside me,
My fancy fled to the South again.

TO THE REV. F. D. MAURICE

COME, when no graver cares employ,
  Godfather, come and see your boy:
    Your presence will be sun in winter,
Making the little one leap for joy.

For, being of that honest few,
Who give the Fiend himself his due,
  Should eighty-thousand college-councils
Thunder 'Anathema', friend, at you;

Should all our churchmen foam in spite
At you, so careful of the right,
  Yet one lay-hearth would give you welcome
(Take it and come) to the Isle of Wight;

Where, far from noise and smoke of town,
I watch the twilight falling brown
  All round a careless-order'd garden
Close to the ridge of a noble down.

You'll have no scandal while you dine,
But honest talk and wholesome wine,
  And only hear the magpie gossip
Garrulous under a roof of pine:

For groves of pine on either hand,
To break the blast of winter, stand;
  And further on, the hoary Channel
Tumbles a billow on chalk and sand;

Where, if below the milky steep
Some ship of battle slowly creep,
  And on thro' zones of light and shadow
Glimmer away to the lonely deep,

We might discuss the Northern sin
Which made a selfish war begin;
    Dispute the claims, arrange the chances;
Emperor, Ottoman, which shall win:

Or whether war's avenging rod
Shall lash all Europe into blood;
    Till you should turn to dearer matters,
Dear to the man that is dear to God;

How best to help the slender store,
How mend the dwellings, of the poor;
    How gain in life, as life advances,
Valour and charity more and more.

Come Maurice, come: the lawn as yet
Is hoar with rime, or spongy-wet;
    But when the wreath of March has blossom'd,
Crocus, anemone, violet,

Or later, pay one visit here,
For those are few we hold as dear;
    Nor pay but one, but come for many,
Many and many a happy year.

IN THE VALLEY OF CAUTERETZ

ALL along the valley, stream that flashest white,
    Deepening thy voice with the deepening of the night,
    All along the valley, where thy waters flow,
I walk'd with one I loved two and thirty years ago.
All along the valley, while I walk'd to-day,
The two and thirty years were a mist that rolls away;

For all along the valley, down thy rocky bed,
Thy living voice to me was as the voice of the dead,
And all along the valley, by rock and cave and tree,
The voice of the dead was a living voice to me.

IN THE GARDEN AT SWAINSTON

NIGHTINGALES warbled without,
   Within was weeping for thee:
   Shadows of three dead men
  Walk'd in the walks with me,
  Shadows of three dead men and thou wast one of the three.

Nightingales sang in his woods:
  The Master was far away:
Nightingales warbled and sang
  Of a passion that lasts but a day;
  Still in the house in his coffin the Prince of courtesy lay.

Two dead men have I known
  In courtesy like to thee:
Two dead men have I loved
  With a love that ever will be:
  Three dead men have I loved and thou art last of the three.

REQUIESCAT

FAIR is her cottage in its place,
   Where yon broad water sweetly slowly glides.
   It sees itself from thatch to base
  Dream in the sliding tides.

And fairer she, but ah how soon to die!
    Her quiet dream of life this hour may cease.
Her peaceful being slowly passes by
    To some more perfect peace.

'FLOWER IN THE CRANNIED WALL'

Flower in the crannied wall,
I pluck you out of the crannies,
I hold you here, root and all, in my hand,
Little flower—but *if* I could understand
What you are, root and all, and all in all,
I should know what God and man is.

SPECIMEN OF A TRANSLATION OF THE ILIAD IN BLANK VERSE

*   *   *

As when in heaven the stars about the moon
    Look beautiful, when all the winds are laid,
And every height comes out, and jutting peak
And valley, and the immeasurable heavens
Break open to their highest, and all the stars
Shine, and the Shepherd gladdens in his heart:
So many a fire between the ships and stream
Of Xanthus blazed before the towers of Troy.

*   *   *

ENOCH ARDEN

*   *   *

                                    She heard,
Heard and not heard him; as the village girl,
Who sets her pitcher underneath the spring,
Musing on him that used to fill it for her,
Hears and not hears, and lets it overflow.

*   *   *

The mountain wooded to the peak, the lawns
And winding glades high up like ways to Heaven,
The slender coco's drooping crown of plumes,
The lightning flash of insect and of bird,
The lustre of the long convolvuluses
That coil'd around the stately stems, and ran
Ev'n to the limit of the land, the glows
And glories of the broad belt of the world,
All these he saw; but what he fain had seen
He could not see, the kindly human face,
Nor ever hear a kindly voice, but heard
The myriad shriek of wheeling ocean-fowl,
The league-long roller thundering on the reef,
The moving whisper of huge trees that branch'd
And blossom'd in the zenith, or the sweep
Of some precipitous rivulet to the wave,
As down the shore he ranged, or all day long
Sat often in the seaward-gazing gorge,
A shipwreck'd sailor, waiting for a sail:
No sail from day to day, but every day
The sunrise broken into scarlet shafts
Among the palms and ferns and precipices;
The blaze upon the waters to the east;
The blaze upon his island overhead;
The blaze upon the waters to the west;
Then the great stars that globed themselves in Heaven,
The hollower-bellowing ocean, and again
The scarlet shafts of sunrise—but no sail.

There often as he watch'd or seem'd to watch,
So still, the golden lizard on him paused,
A phantom made of many phantoms moved

Before him haunting him, or he himself
Moved haunting people, things and places, known
Far in a darker isle beyond the line;
The babes, their babble, Annie, the small house,
The climbing street, the mill, the leafy lanes,
The peacock-yewtree and the lonely Hall,
The horse he drove, the boat he sold, the chill
November dawns and dewy-glooming downs,
The gentle shower, the smell of dying leaves,
And the low moan of leaden-colour'd seas.

* * *

              Bright was that afternoon,
Sunny but chill; till drawn thro' either chasm,
Where either haven open'd on the deeps,
Roll'd a sea-haze and whelm'd the world in gray;
Cut off the length of highway on before,
And left but narrow breadth to left and right
Of wither'd holt or tilth or pasturage.
On the nigh-naked tree the robin piped
Disconsolate, and thro' the dripping haze
The dead weight of the dead leaf bore it down:
Thicker the drizzle grew, deeper the gloom;
Last, as it seem'd, a great mist-blotted light
Flared on him, and he came upon the place.

* * *

AYLMER'S FIELD

* * *

              Sketches rude and faint,
But where a passion yet unborn perhaps
Lay hidden as the music of the moon
Sleeps in the plain eggs of the nightingale.

* * *

Then the great Hall was wholly broken down,
And the broad woodland parcell'd into farms;
And where the two contrived their daughter's good,
Lies the hawk's cast, the mole has made his run,
The hedgehog underneath the plantain bores,
The rabbit fondles his own harmless face,
The slow-worm creeps, and the thin weasel there
Follows the mouse, and all is open field.

LUCRETIUS

LUCILIA, wedded to Lucretius, found
Her master cold; for when the morning flush
Of passion and the first embrace had died
Between them, tho' he lov'd her none the less,
Yet often when the woman heard his foot
Return from pacings in the field, and ran
To greet him with a kiss, the master took
Small notice, or austerely, for—his mind
Half buried in some weightier argument,
Or fancy-borne perhaps upon the rise
And long roll of the Hexameter—he past
To turn and ponder those three hundred scrolls
Left by the Teacher, whom he held divine.
She brook'd it not; but wrathful, petulant,
Dreaming some rival, sought and found a witch
Who brew'd the philtre which had power, they said,
To lead an errant passion home again.
And this, at times, she mingled with his drink,
And this destroy'd him; for the wicked broth
Confused the chemic labour of the blood,

And tickling the brute brain within the man's
Made havock among those tender cells, and check'd
His power to shape: he loathed himself; and once
After a tempest woke upon a morn
That mock'd him with returning calm, and cried:

  'Storm in the night! for thrice I heard the rain
Rushing; and once the flash of a thunderbolt—
Methought I never saw so fierce a fork—
Struck out the streaming mountain-side, and show'd
A riotous confluence of watercourses
Blanching and billowing in a hollow of it,
Where all but yester-eve was dusty-dry.

  'Storm, and what dreams, ye holy Gods, what dreams!
For thrice I waken'd after dreams. Perchance
We do but recollect the dreams that come
Just ere the waking: terrible! for it seem'd
A void was made in Nature; all her bonds
Crack'd; and I saw the flaring atom-streams
And torrents of her myriad universe,
Ruining along the illimitable inane,
Fly on to clash together again, and make
Another and another frame of things
For ever: that was mine, my dream, I knew it—
Of and belonging to me, as the dog
With inward yelp and restless forefoot plies
His function of the woodland: but the next!
I thought that all the blood by Sylla shed
Came driving rainlike down again on earth,
And where it dash'd the reddening meadow, sprang
No dragon warriors from Cadmean teeth,
For these I thought my dream would show to me,

But girls, Hetairai, curious in their art,
Hired animalisms, vile as those that made
The mulberry-faced Dictator's orgies worse
Than aught they fable of the quiet Gods.
And hands they mixt, and yell'd and round me drove
In narrowing circles till I yell'd again
Half-suffocated, and sprang up, and saw—
Was it the first beam of my latest day?

'Then, then, from utter gloom stood out the breasts,
The breasts of Helen, and hoveringly a sword
Now over and now under, now direct,
Pointed itself to pierce, but sank down shamed
At all that beauty; and as I stared, a fire,
The fire that left a roofless Ilion,
Shot out of them, and scorch'd me that I woke.

'Is this thy vengeance, holy Venus, thine,
Because I would not one of thine own doves,
Not ev'n a rose, were offer'd to thee? thine,
Forgetful how my rich procemion makes
Thy glory fly along the Italian field,
In lays that will outlast thy Deity?

'Deity? nay, thy worshippers. My tongue
Trips, or I speak profanely. Which of these
Angers thee most, or angers thee at all?
Not if thou be'st of those who, far aloof
From envy, hate and pity, and spite and scorn,
Live the great life which all our greatest fain
Would follow, center'd in eternal calm.

'Nay, if thou canst, O Goddess, like ourselves
Touch, and be touch'd, then would I cry to thee

To kiss thy Mavors, roll thy tender arms
Round him, and keep him from the lust of blood
That makes a steaming slaughter-house of Rome.

  'Ay, but I meant not thee; I meant not her,
Whom all the pines of Ida shook to see
Slide from that quiet heaven of hers, and tempt
The Trojan, while his neat-herds were abroad;
Nor her that o'er her wounded hunter wept
Her Deity false in human-amorous tears;
Nor whom her beardless apple-arbiter
Decided fairest. Rather, O ye Gods,
Poet-like, as the great Sicilian called
Calliope to grace his golden verse—
Ay, and this Kypris also—did I take
That popular name of thine to shadow forth
The all-generating powers and genial heat
Of Nature, when she strikes thro' the thick blood
Of cattle, and light is large, and lambs are glad
Nosing the mother's udder, and the bird
Makes his heart voice amid the blaze of flowers:
Which things appear the work of mighty Gods.

  'The Gods! and if I go *my* work is left
Unfinish'd—*if* I go. The Gods, who haunt
The lucid interspace of world and world,
Where never creeps a cloud, or moves a wind,
Nor ever falls the least white star of snow,
Nor ever lowest roll of thunder moans,
Nor sound of human sorrow mounts to mar
Their sacred everlasting calm! and such,
Not all so fine, nor so divine a calm,

Not such, nor all unlike it, man may gain
Letting his own life go. The Gods, the Gods!
If all be atoms, how then should the Gods
Being atomic not be dissoluble,
Not follow the great law? My Master held
That Gods there are, for all men so believe.
I prest my footsteps into his, and meant
Surely to lead my Memmius in a train
Of flowery clauses onward to the proof
That Gods there are, and deathless. Meant? I meant?
I have forgotten what I meant: my mind
Stumbles, and all my faculties are lamed.

'Look where another of our Gods, the Sun,
Apollo, Delius, or of older use
All-seeing Hyperion—what you will—
Has mounted yonder; since he never sware,
Except his wrath were wreak'd on wretched man,
That he would only shine among the dead
Hereafter; tales! for never yet on earth
Could dead flesh creep, or bits of roasting ox
Moan round the spit—nor knows he what he sees;
King of the East altho' he seem, and girt
With song and flame and fragrance, slowly lifts
His golden feet on those empurpled stairs
That climb into the windy halls of Heaven:
And here he glances on an eye new-born,
And gets for greeting but a wail of pain;
And here he stays upon a freezing orb
That fain would gaze upon him to the last;
And here upon a yellow eyelid fall'n
And closed by those who mourn a friend in vain,

Not thankful that his troubles are no more.
And me, altho' his fire is on my face
Blinding, he sees not, nor at all can tell
Whether I mean this day to end myself,
Or lend an ear to Plato where he says,
That men like soldiers may not quit the post
Allotted by the Gods: but he that holds
The Gods are careless, wherefore need he care
Greatly for them, nor rather plunge at once,
Being troubled, wholly out of sight, and sink
Past earthquake—ay, and gout and stone, that break
Body toward death, and palsy, death-in-life,
And wretched age—and worst disease of all,
These prodigies of myriad nakednesses,
And twisted shapes of lust, unspeakable,
Abominable, strangers at my hearth
Not welcome, harpies miring every dish,
The phantom husks of something foully done,
And fleeting thro' the boundless universe,
And blasting the long quiet of my breast
With animal heat and dire insanity?

'How should the mind, except it loved them, clasp
These idols to herself? or do they fly
Now thinner, and now thicker, like the flakes
In a fall of snow, and so press in, perforce
Of multitude, as crowds that in an hour
Of civic tumult jam the doors, and bear
The keepers down, and throng, their rags and they
The basest, far into that council-hall
Where sit the best and stateliest of the land?

'Can I not fling this horror off me again,
Seeing with how great ease Nature can smile,
Balmier and nobler from her bath of storm,
At random ravage? and how easily
The mountain there has cast his cloudy slough,
Now towering o'er him in serenest air,
A mountain o'er a mountain,—ay, and within
All hollow as the hopes and fears of men?

'But who was he, that in the garden snared
Picus and Faunus, rustic Gods? a tale
To laugh at—more to laugh at in myself—
For look! what is it? there? yon arbutus
Totters; a noiseless riot underneath
Strikes through the wood, sets all the tops quivering—
The mountain quickens into Nymph and Faun;
And here an Oread—how the sun delights
To glance and shift about her slippery sides,
And rosy knees and supple roundedness,
And budded bosom-peaks—who this way runs
Before the rest—A satyr, a satyr, see,
Follows; but him I proved impossible;
Twy-natured is no nature: yet he draws
Nearer and nearer, and I scan him now
Beastlier than any phantom of his kind
That ever butted his rough brother-brute
For lust or lusty blood or provender:
I hate, abhor, spit, sicken at him; and she
Loathes him as well; such a precipitate heel,
Fledged as it were with Mercury's ankle-wing,
Whirls her to me: but will she fling herself,
Shameless upon me? Catch her, goat-foot: nay,

Hide, hide them, million-myrtled wilderness,
And cavern-shadowing laurels, hide! do I wish—
What?—that the bush were leafless? or to whelm
All of them in one massacre? O ye Gods,
I know you careless, yet, behold, to you
From childly wont and ancient use I call—
I thought I lived securely as yourselves—
No lewdness, narrowing envy, monkey-spite,
No madness of ambition, avarice, none:
No larger feast than under plane or pine
With neighbours laid along the grass, to take
Only such cups as left us friendly-warm,
Affirming each his own philosophy—
Nothing to mar the sober majesties
Of settled, sweet, Epicurean life.
But now it seems some unseen monster lays
His vast and filthy hands upon my will,
Wrenching it backward into his; and spoils
My bliss in being; and it was not great;
For save when shutting reasons up in rhythm,
Or Heliconian honey in living words,
To make a truth less harsh, I often grew
Tired of so much within our little life,
Or of so little in our little life—
Poor little life that toddles half an hour
Crown'd with a flower or two, and there an end—
And since the nobler pleasure seems to fade,
Why should I, beastlike as I find myself,
Not manlike end myself?—our privilege—
What beast has heart to do it? And what man,
What Roman would be dragg'd in triumph thus?
Not I; not he, who bears one name with her

Whose death-blow struck the dateless doom of kings,
When, brooking not the Tarquin in her veins,
She made her blood in sight of Collatine
And all his peers, flushing the guiltless air,
Spout from the maiden fountain in her heart.
And from it sprang the Commonwealth, which breaks
As I am breaking now!

     'And therefore now
Let her, that is the womb and tomb of all,
Great Nature, take, and forcing far apart
Those blind beginnings that have made me man,
Dash them anew together at her will
Thro' all her cycles—into man once more,
Or beast or bird or fish, or opulent flower:
But till this cosmic order everywhere
Shatter'd into one earthquake in one day
Cracks all to pieces,—and that hour perhaps
Is not so far when momentary man
Shall seem no more a something to himself,
But he, his hopes and hates, his homes and fanes,
And even his bones long laid within the grave,
The very sides of the grave itself shall pass,
Vanishing, atom and void, atom and void,
Into the unseen for ever,—till that hour,
My golden work in which I told a truth
That stays the rolling Ixionian wheel,
And numbs the Fury's ringlet-snake, and plucks
The mortal soul from out immortal hell,
Shall stand: ay, surely: then it fails at last
And perishes as I must; for O Thou,
Passionless bride, divine Tranquillity,

Yearn'd after by the wisest of the wise,
Who fail to find thee, being as thou art
Without one pleasure and without one pain,
Howbeit I know thou surely must be mine
Or soon or late, yet out of season, thus
I woo thee roughly, for thou carest not
How roughly men may woo thee so they win—
Thus—thus: the soul flies out and dies in the air.'

With that he drove the knife into his side:
She heard him raging, heard him fall; ran in,
Beat breast, tore hair, cried out upon herself
As having fail'd in duty to him, shriek'd
That she but meant to win him back, fell on him,
Clasp'd, kiss'd him, wail'd: he answer'd, 'Care not thou!
Thy duty? What is duty? Fare thee well!'

IDYLLS OF THE KING

THE COMING OF ARTHUR

THE TALE OF BLEYS

*   *   *

'But let me tell thee now another tale:
For Bleys, our Merlin's master, as they say,
Died but of late, and sent his cry to me,
To hear him speak before he left his life.
Shrunk like a fairy changeling lay the mage;
And when I enter'd told me that himself
And Merlin ever served about the King,
Uther, before he died; and on the night

When Uther in Tintagil past away
Moaning and wailing for an heir, the two
Left the still King, and passing forth to breathe,
Then from the castle gateway by the chasm
Descending thro' the dismal night—a night
In which the bounds of heaven and earth were lost—
Beheld, so high upon the dreary deeps
It seem'd in heaven, a ship, the shape thereof
A dragon wing'd, and all from stem to stern
Bright with a shining people on the decks,
And gone as soon as seen. And then the two
Dropt to the cove, and watch'd the great sea fall,
Wave after wave, each mightier than the last,
Till last, a ninth one, gathering half the deep
And full of voices, slowly rose and plunged
Roaring, and all the wave was in a flame:
And down the wave and in the flame was borne
A naked babe, and rode to Merlin's feet,
Who stoopt and caught the babe, and cried "The King!
Here is an heir for Uther!" And the fringe
Of that great breaker, sweeping up the strand,
Lash'd at the wizard as he spake the word,
And all at once all round him rose in fire,
So that the child and he were clothed in fire.
And presently thereafter follow'd calm,
Free sky and stars: "And this same child", he said,
"Is he who reigns; nor could I part in peace
Till this were told". And saying this the seer
Went thro' the strait and dreadful pass of death.
Not ever to be question'd any more
Save on the further side.'

*　　　*　　　*

GARETH AND LYNETTE

GARETH'S FIRST ADVENTURE
* * *

So till the dusk that follow'd evensong
   Rode on the two, reviler and reviled;
   Then after one long slope was mounted, saw,
Bowl-shaped, thro' tops of many thousand pines
A gloomy-gladed hollow slowly sink
To westward—in the deeps whereof a mere,
Round as the red eye of an Eagle-owl,
Under the half-dead sunset glared; and shouts
Ascended, and there brake a servingman
Flying from out of the black wood, and crying,
'They have bound my lord to cast him in the mere'.

* * *

GERAINT AND ENID

THE MEETING OF GERAINT AND ENID
* * *

Then rode Geraint into the castle court,
   His charger trampling many a prickly star
   Of sprouted thistle on the broken stones.
He look'd and saw that all was ruinous.
Here stood a shatter'd archway plumed with fern;
And here had fall'n a great part of a tower,
Whole, like a crag that tumbles from the cliff,
And like a crag was gay with wilding flowers:
And high above a piece of turret stair,
Worn by the feet that now were silent, wound
Bare to the sun, and monstrous ivy-stems

Claspt the gray walls with hairy-fibred arms,
And suck'd the joining of the stones, and look'd
A knot, beneath, of snakes, aloft, a grove.

And while he waited in the castle court,
The voice of Enid, Yniol's daughter, rang
Clear thro' the open casement of the hall,
Singing; and as the sweet voice of a bird,
Heard by the lander in a lonely isle,
Moves him to think what kind of bird it is
That sings so delicately clear, and make
Conjecture of the plumage and the form;
So the sweet voice of Enid moved Geraint;
And made him like a man abroad at morn
When first the liquid note beloved of men
Comes flying over many a windy wave
To Britain, and in April suddenly
Breaks from a coppice gemm'd with green and red,
And he suspends his converse with a friend,
Or it may be the labour of his hands,
To think or say, 'There is the nightingale';
So fared it with Geraint, who thought and said,
'Here, by God's grace, is the one voice for me'.

* * *

GERAINT SCATTERS THE FOLLOWERS OF LIMOURS

* * *

But at the flash and motion of the man
They vanish'd panic-stricken, like a shoal
Of darting fish, that on a summer morn
Adown the crystal dykes at Camelot
Come slipping o'er their shadows on the sand,

But if a man who stands upon the brink
But lift a shining hand against the sun,
There is not left the twinkle of a fin
Betwixt the cressy islets white in flower.

* * *

THEIR RECONCILIATION

    And never yet, since high in Paradise
O'er the four rivers the first roses blew,
Came purer pleasure unto mortal kind
Than lived thro' her, who in that perilous hour
Put hand to hand beneath her husband's heart,
And felt him hers again: she did not weep,
But o'er her meek eyes came a happy mist
Like that which kept the heart of Eden green
Before the useful trouble of the rain.

* * *

MERLIN AND VIVIEN

MERLIN'S FOREBODING

* * *

              He was mute:
So dark a forethought roll'd about his brain,
As on a dull day in an Ocean cave
The blind wave feeling round his long sea-hall
In silence.

* * *

    And Merlin lock'd his hand in hers and said:
'O did ye never lie upon the shore,
And watch the curl'd white of the coming wave

Glass'd in the slippery sand before it breaks?
Ev'n such a wave, but not so pleasurable,
Dark in the glass of some presageful mood,
Had I for three days seen, ready to fall'.

* * *

THE DAWN OF ARTHUR'S REIGN

And Merlin look'd and half believed her true,
So tender was her voice, so fair her face,
So sweetly gleam'd her eyes behind her tears
Like sunlight on the plain behind a shower:
And yet he answer'd half indignantly:

'Far other was the song that once I heard
By this huge oak, sung nearly where we sit:
For here we met, some ten or twelve of us,
To chase a creature that was current then
In these wild woods, the hart with golden horns.
It was the time when first the question rose
About the founding of a Table Round,
That was to be, for love of God and men
And noble deeds, the flower of all the world.
And each incited each to noble deeds.
And while we waited, one, the youngest of us,
We could not keep him silent, out he flash'd,
And into such a song, such fire for fame,
Such trumpet-blowings in it, coming down
To such a stern and iron-clashing close,
That when he stopt we long'd to hurl together,
And should have done it; but the beauteous beast
Scared by the noise upstarted at our feet,

And like a silver shadow slipt away
Thro' the dim land; and all day long we rode
Thro' the dim land against a rushing wind,
That glorious roundel echoing in our ears,
And chased the flashes of his golden horns
Until they vanish'd by the fairy well
That laughs at iron—as our warriors did—
Where children cast their pins and nails, and cry,
"Laugh, little well!" but touch it with a sword,
It buzzes fiercely round the point; and there
We lost him: such a noble song was that.
But, Vivien, when you sang me that sweet rhyme,
I felt as tho' you knew this cursed charm,
Were proving it on me, and that I lay
And felt them slowly ebbing, name and fame'.

* * *

VIVIEN'S SONG

    This rhyme
Is like the fair pearl-necklace of the Queen,
That burst in dancing, and the pearls were spilt;
Some lost, some stolen, some as relics kept.
But nevermore the same two sister pearls
Ran down the silken thread to kiss each other
On her white neck—so is it with this rhyme:
It lives dispersedly in many hands,
And every minstrel sings it differently.

* * *

THE EMPTINESS OF FAME

                That other fame,
To one at least, who hath not children, vague,
The cackle of the unborn about the grave,
I cared not for it: a single misty star,
Which is the second in a line of stars
That seem a sword beneath a belt of three,
I never gazed upon it but I dreamt
Of some vast charm concluded in that star
To make fame nothing.

     *   *   *

THE TALE OF MERLIN'S SPELL

    Then the great Master merrily answer'd her:
'Full many a love in loving youth was mine;
I needed then no charm to keep them mine
But youth and love; and that full heart of yours
Whereof ye prattle, may now assure you mine;
So live uncharm'd. For those who wrought it first,
The wrist is parted from the hand that waved,
The feet unmortised from their ankle-bones
Who paced it, ages back: but will ye hear
The legend as in guerdon for your rhyme?

    'There lived a king in the most Eastern East,
Less old than I, yet older, for my blood
Hath earnest in it of far springs to be.
A tawny pirate anchor'd in his port,
Whose bark had plunder'd twenty nameless isles;
And passing one, at the high peep of dawn,

He saw two cities in a thousand boats
All fighting for a woman on the sea.
And pushing his black craft among them all,
He lightly scatter'd theirs and brought her off,
With loss of half his people arrow-slain;
A maid so smooth, so white, so wonderful,
They said a light came from her when she moved:
And since the pirate would not yield her up,
The King impaled him for his piracy;
Then made her Queen: but those isle-nurtured eyes
Waged such unwilling tho' successful war
On all the youth, they sicken'd; councils thinn'd,
And armies waned, for magnet-like she drew
The rustiest iron of old fighters' hearts;
And beasts themselves would worship; camels knelt
Unbidden, and the brutes of mountain back
That carry kings in castles, bow'd black knees
Of homage, ringing with their serpent hands,
To make her smile, her golden ankle-bells.
What wonder, being jealous, that he sent
His horns of proclamation out thro' all
The hundred under-kingdoms that he sway'd
To find a wizard who might teach the King
Some charm, which being wrought upon the Queen
Might keep her all his own? To such a one
He promised more than ever king has given,
A league of mountain full of golden mines,
A province with a hundred miles of coast,
A palace and a princess, all for him:
But on all those who tried and fail'd, the King
Pronounced a dismal sentence, meaning by it
To keep the list low and pretenders back,

Or, like a king, not to be trifled with—
Their heads should moulder on the city gates.
And many tried and fail'd, because the charm
Of nature in her overbore their own:
And many a wizard brow bleach'd on the walls:
And many weeks a troop of carrion crows
Hung like a cloud above the gateway towers'.

And Vivien breaking in upon him, said:
'I sit and gather honey; yet, methinks,
Thy tongue has tript a little: ask thyself.
The lady never made *unwilling* war
With those fine eyes: she had her pleasure in it,
And made her good man jealous with good cause.
And lived there neither dame nor damsel then
Wroth at a lover's loss? were all as tame,
I mean, as noble, as their Queen was fair?
Not one to flirt a venom at her eyes,
Or pinch a murderous dust into her drink,
Or make her paler with a poison'd rose?
Well, those were not our days: but did they find
A wizard? Tell me, was he like to thee?'

She ceased, and made her lithe arm round his neck
Tighten, and then drew back, and let her eyes
Speak for her, glowing on him, like a bride's
On her new lord, her own, the first of men.

He answer'd laughing, 'Nay, not like to me.
At last they found—his foragers for charms—
A little glassy-headed hairless man,
Who lived alone in a great wild on grass;

Read but one book, and ever reading grew
So grated down and filed away with thought,
So lean, his eyes were monstrous; while the skin
Clung but to crate and basket, ribs and spine.
And since he kept his mind on one sole aim,
Nor ever touch'd fierce wine, nor tasted flesh,
Nor own'd a sensual wish, to him the wall
That sunders ghosts and shadow-casting men
Became a crystal, and he saw them thro' it,
And heard their voices talk behind the wall,
And learnt their elemental secrets, powers
And forces; often o'er the sun's bright eye
Drew the vast eyelid of an inky cloud,
And lash'd it at the base with slanting storm;
Or in the noon of mist and driving rain,
When the lake whiten'd and the pinewood roar'd,
And the cairn'd mountain was a shadow, sunn'd
The world to peace again: here was the man.
And so by force they dragg'd him to the King.
And then he taught the King to charm the Queen
In such-wise, that no man could see her more,
Nor saw she save the King, who wrought the charm,
Coming and going, and she lay as dead,
And lost all use of life: but when the King
Made proffer of the league of golden mines,
The province with a hundred miles of coast,
The palace and the princess, that old man
Went back to his old wild, and lived on grass,
And vanish'd, and his book came down to me'.

*   *   *

MERLIN'S FALL

The pale blood of the wizard at her touch
Took gayer colours, like an opal warm'd.
She blamed herself for telling hearsay tales:
She shook from fear, and for her fault she wept
Of petulancy; she call'd him lord and liege,
Her seer, her bard, her silver star of eve,
Her God, her Merlin, the one passionate love
Of her whole life; and ever overhead
Bellow'd the tempest, and the rotten branch
Snapt in the rushing of the river-rain
Above them; and in change of glare and gloom
Her eyes and neck glittering went and came;
Till now the storm, its burst of passion spent,
Moaning and calling out of other lands,
Had left the ravaged woodland yet once more
To peace; and what should not have been had been,
For Merlin, overtalk'd and overworn,
Had yielded, told her all the charm, and slept.

Then in one moment, she put forth the charm
Of woven paces and of waving hands,
And in the hollow oak he lay as dead,
And lost to life and use and name and fame.

Then crying 'I have made his glory mine',
And shrieking out 'O fool!' the harlot leapt
Adown the forest, and the thicket closed
Behind her, and the forest echo'd 'fool'.

LANCELOT AND ELAINE

THE FINDING OF THE DIAMONDS OF THE TOURNAMENT

*   *   *

For Arthur, long before they crown'd him King,
Roving the trackless realms of Lyonnesse,
Had found a glen, gray boulder and black tarn.
A horror lived about the tarn, and clave
Like its own mists to all the mountain side:
For here two brothers, one a king, had met
And fought together; but their names were lost;
And each had slain his brother at a blow;
And down they fell and made the glen abhorr'd:
And there they lay till all their bones were bleach'd,
And lichen'd into colour with the crags:
And he, that once was king, had on a crown
Of diamonds, one in front, and four aside.
And Arthur came, and labouring up the pass,
All in a misty moonshine, unawares
Had trodden that crown'd skeleton, and the skull
Brake from the nape, and from the skull the crown
Roll'd into light, and turning on its rims
Fled like a glittering rivulet to the tarn:
And down the shingly scaur he plunged, and caught,
And set it on his head, and in his heart
Heard murmurs, 'Lo, thou likewise shalt be King'.

*   *   *

GUINEVERE ON ARTHUR

She broke into a little scornful laugh:
'Arthur, my lord, Arthur, the faultless King,

That passionate perfection, my good lord—
But who can gaze upon the Sun in heaven?
He never spake word of reproach to me,
He never had a glimpse of mine untruth,
He cares not for me: only here to-day
There gleam'd a vague suspicion in his eyes:
Some meddling rogue has tamper'd with him—else
Rapt in this fancy of his Table Round,
And swearing men to vows impossible,
To make them like himself: but, friend, to me
He is all fault who hath no fault at all:
For who loves me must have a touch of earth;
The low sun makes the colour: I am yours'.

* * *

SIR LANCELOT'S KINDRED RIDE HIM DOWN

They couch'd their spears and prick'd their steeds, and thus,
Their plumes driv'n backward by the wind they made
In moving, all together down upon him
Bare, as a wild wave in the wild North-sea,
Green-glimmering toward the summit, bears, with all
Its stormy crests that smoke against the skies,
Down on a bark, and overbears the bark,
And him that helms it, so they overbore
Sir Lancelot and his charger, and a spear
Down-glancing lamed the charger, and a spear
Prick'd sharply his own cuirass, and the head
Pierced thro' his side, and there snapt, and remain'd.

* * *

THE END OF ELAINE
* * *
     Full meekly rose the maid,
Stript off the case, and gave the naked shield;
Then, when she heard his horse upon the stones,
Unclasping flung the casement back, and look'd
Down on his helm, from which her sleeve had gone.
And Lancelot knew the little clinking sound;
And she by tact of love was well aware
That Lancelot knew that she was looking at him.
And yet he glanced not up, nor waved his hand,
Nor bad farewell, but sadly rode away.
This was the one discourtesy that he used.

 So in her tower alone the maiden sat:
His very shield was gone; only the case,
Her own poor work, her empty labour, left.
But still she heard him, still his picture form'd
And grew between her and the pictured wall.
Then came her father, saying in low tones,
'Have comfort', whom she greeted quietly.
Then came her brethren saying, 'Peace to thee,
Sweet sister', whom she answer'd with all calm.
But when they left her to herself again,
Death, like a friend's voice from a distant field
Approaching thro' the darkness, call'd; the owls
Wailing had power upon her, and she mixt
Her fancies with the sallow-rifted glooms
Of evening, and the moanings of the wind.

 And in those days she made a little song,
And call'd her song 'The Song of Love and Death',
And sang it: sweetly could she make and sing.

'Sweet is true love tho' given in vain, in vain;
And sweet is death who puts an end to pain:
I know not which is sweeter, no, not I.

'Love, art thou sweet? then bitter death must be:
Love, thou art bitter; sweet is death to me.
O Love, if death be sweeter, let me die.

'Sweet love, that seems not made to fade away,
Sweet death, that seems to make us loveless clay,
I know not which is sweeter, no, not I.

'I fain would follow love, if that could be;
I needs must follow death, who calls for me;
Call and I follow, I follow! let me die.'

High with the last line scaled her voice, and this,
All in a fiery dawning wild with wind
That shook her tower, the brothers heard, and thought
With shuddering, 'Hark the Phantom of the house
That ever shrieks before a death', and call'd
The father, and all three in hurry and fear
Ran to her, and lo! the blood-red light of dawn
Flared on her face, she shrilling, 'Let me die!'

As when we dwell upon a word we know,
Repeating, till the word we know so well
Becomes a wonder, and we know not why,
So dwelt the father on her face, and thought
'Is this Elaine?' till back the maiden fell,
Then gave a languid hand to each, and lay,
Speaking a still good-morrow with her eyes.
At last she said, 'Sweet brothers, yesternight
I seem'd a curious little maid again,

As happy as when we dwelt among the woods,
And when ye used to take me with the flood
Up the great river in the boatman's boat.
Only ye would not pass beyond the cape
That has the poplar on it: there ye fixt
Your limit, oft returning with the tide.
And yet I cried because ye would not pass
Beyond it, and far up the shining flood
Until we found the palace of the King.
And yet ye would not; but this night I dream'd
That I was all alone upon the flood,
And then I said, "Now shall I have my will":
And there I woke, but still the wish remain'd.
So let me hence that I may pass at last
Beyond the poplar and far up the flood,
Until I find the palace of the King.
There will I enter in among them all,
And no man there will dare to mock at me;
But there the fine Gawain will wonder at me,
And there the great Sir Lancelot muse at me;
Gawain, who bad a thousand farewells to me,
Lancelot, who coldly went, nor bad me one:
And there the King will know me and my love,
And there the Queen herself will pity me,
And all the gentle court will welcome me,
And after my long voyage I shall rest!'

* * *

SIR LANCELOT'S REMORSE

And Lancelot answer'd nothing, but he went,
And at the inrunning of a little brook

Sat by the river in a cove, and watch'd
The high reed wave, and lifted up his eyes
And saw the barge that brought her moving down,
Far-off, a blot upon the stream, and said
Low in himself, 'Ah simple heart and sweet,
Ye loved me, damsel, surely with a love
Far tenderer than my Queen's. Pray for thy soul?
Ay, that will I. Farewell too—now at last—
Farewell, fair lily. "Jealousy in love?"
Not rather dead love's harsh heir, jealous pride?
Queen, if I grant the jealousy as of love,
May not your crescent fear for name and fame
Speak, as it waxes, of a love that wanes?
Why did the King dwell on my name to me?
Mine own name shames me, seeming a reproach,
Lancelot, whom the Lady of the Lake
Caught from his mother's arms—the wondrous one
Who passes thro' the vision of the night—
She chanted snatches of mysterious hymns
Heard on the winding waters, eve and morn
She kiss'd me saying, "Thou art fair, my child,
As a king's son", and often in her arms
She bare me, pacing on the dusky mere.
Would she had drown'd me in it, where'er it be!
For what am I? what profits me my name
Of greatest knight? I fought for it, and have it:
Pleasure to have it, none; to lose it, pain;
Now grown a part of me: but what use in it?
To make men worse by making my sin known?
Or sin seem less, the sinner seeming great?
Alas for Arthur's greatest knight, a man
Not after Arthur's heart! I needs must break

These bonds that so defame me: not without
She wills it: would I, if she will'd it? nay,
Who knows? but if I would not, then may God,
I pray him, send a sudden Angel down
To seize me by the hair and bear me far,
And fling me deep in that forgotten mere,
Among the tumbled fragments of the hills'.

So groan'd Sir Lancelot in remorseful pain,
Not knowing he should die a holy man.

THE HOLY GRAIL

ARTHUR'S HALL

* * *

'O BROTHER, had you known our mighty hall,
Which Merlin built for Arthur long ago!
For all the sacred mount of Camelot,
And all the dim rich city, roof by roof,
Tower after tower, spire beyond spire,
By grove, and garden-lawn, and rushing brook,
Climbs to the mighty hall that Merlin built.
And four great zones of sculpture, set betwixt
With many a mystic symbol, gird the hall:
And in the lowest beasts are slaying men,
And in the second men are slaying beasts,
And on the third are warriors, perfect men,
And on the fourth are men with growing wings,
And over all one statue in the mould
Of Arthur, made by Merlin, with a crown,
And peak'd wings pointed to the Northern Star.
And eastward fronts the statue, and the crown

And both the wings are made of gold, and flame
At sunrise till the people in far fields,
Wasted so often by the heathen hordes,
Behold it, crying, "We have still a King".

'And, brother, had you known our hall within,
Broader and higher than any in all the lands!
Where twelve great windows blazon Arthur's wars,
And all the light that falls upon the board
Streams thro' the twelve great battles of our King.
Nay, one there is, and at the eastern end,
Wealthy with wandering lines of mount and mere,
Where Arthur finds the brand Excalibur.
And also one to the west, and counter to it,
And blank: and who shall blazon it? when and how?—
O there, perchance, when all our wars are done,
The brand Excalibur will be cast away.'

* * *

ARTHUR'S CITY

'O brother, had you known our Camelot,
Built by old kings, age after age, so old
The King himself had fears that it would fall,
So strange, and rich, and dim; for where the roofs
Totter'd toward each other in the sky,
Met foreheads all along the street of those
Who watch'd us pass; and lower, and where the long
Rich galleries, lady-laden, weigh'd the necks
Of dragons clinging to the crazy walls,
Thicker than drops from thunder, showers of flowers
Fell as we past; and men and boys astride

On wyvern, lion, dragon, griffin, swan,
At all the corners, named us each by name,
Calling "God speed!" but in the ways below
The knights and ladies wept, and rich and poor
Wept, and the King himself could hardly speak
For grief, and all in middle street the Queen,
Who rode by Lancelot, wail'd and shriek'd aloud,
"This madness has come on us for our sins".
So to the Gate of the three Queens we came,
Where Arthur's wars are render'd mystically,
And thence departed every one his way.'

* * *

THE PASSING OF SIR GALAHAD

'There rose a hill that none but man could climb,
Scarr'd with a hundred wintry water-courses—
Storm at the top, and when we gain'd it, storm
Round us and death; for every moment glanced
His silver arms and gloom'd: so quick and thick
The lightnings here and there to left and right
Struck, till the dry old trunks about us, dead,
Yea, rotten with a hundred years of death,
Sprang into fire: and at the base we found
On either hand, as far as eye could see,
A great black swamp and of an evil smell,
Part black, part whiten'd with the bones of men,
Not to be crost, save that some ancient king
Had built a way, where, link'd with many a bridge,
A thousand piers ran into the great Sea.
And Galahad fled along them bridge by bridge,

And every bridge as quickly as he crost
Sprang into fire and vanish'd, tho' I yearn'd
To follow; and thrice above him all the heavens
Open'd and blazed with thunder such as seem'd
Shoutings of all the sons of God: and first
At once I saw him far on the great Sea,
In silver-shining armour starry-clear;
And o'er his head the Holy Vessel hung
Clothed in white samite or a luminous cloud.
And with exceeding swiftness ran the boat,
If boat it were—I saw not whence it came.
And when the heavens open'd and blazed again
Roaring, I saw him like a silver star—
And had he set the sail, or had the boat
Become a living creature clad with wings?
And o'er his head the Holy Vessel hung
Redder than any rose, a joy to me,
For now I knew the veil had been withdrawn.
Then in a moment when they blazed again
Opening, I saw the least of little stars
Down on the waste, and straight beyond the star
I saw the spiritual city and all her spires
And gateways in a glory like one pearl—
No larger, tho' the goal of all the saints—
Strike from the sea; and from the star there shot
A rose-red sparkle to the city, and there
Dwelt, and I knew it was the Holy Grail,
Which never eyes on earth again shall see.
Then fell the floods of heaven drowning the deep.
And how my feet recrost the deathful ridge
No memory in me lives; but that I touch'd
The chapel-doors at dawn I know; and thence

Taking my war-horse from the holy man,
Glad that no phantom vext me more, return'd
To whence I came, the gate of Arthur's wars.'

* * *

SIR LANCELOT'S QUEST FOR THE GRAIL

                    And then I came
All in my folly to the naked shore,
Wide flats, where nothing but coarse grasses grew;
But such a blast, my King, began to blow,
So loud a blast along the shore and sea,
Ye could not hear the waters for the blast,
Tho' heapt in mounds and ridges all the sea
Drove like a cataract, and all the sand
Swept like a river, and the clouded heavens
Were shaken with the motion and the sound.
And blackening in the sea-foam sway'd a boat,
Half-swallow'd in it, anchor'd with a chain;
And in my madness to myself I said,
'I will embark and I will lose myself,
And in the great sea wash away my sin'.
I burst the chain, I sprang into the boat.
Seven days I drove along the dreary deep,
And with me drove the moon and all the stars;
And the wind fell, and on the seventh night
I heard the shingle grinding in the surge,
And felt the boat shock earth, and looking up,
Behold, the enchanted towers of Carbonek,
A castle like a rock upon a rock,
With chasm-like portals open to the sea,
And steps that met the breaker! there was none

Stood near it but a lion on each side
That kept the entry, and the moon was full.
Then from the boat I leapt, and up the stairs.
There drew my sword. With sudden-flaring manes
Those two great beasts rose upright like a man,
Each gript a shoulder, and I stood between;
And, when I would have smitten them, heard a voice,
'Doubt not, go forward; if thou doubt, the beasts
Will tear thee piecemeal'. Then with violence
The sword was dash'd from out my hand, and fell.
And up into the sounding hall I past;
But nothing in the sounding hall I saw,
No bench nor table, painting on the wall
Or shield of knight; only the rounded moon
Thro' the tall oriel on the rolling sea.
But always in the quiet house I heard,
Clear as a lark, high o'er me as a lark,
A sweet voice singing in the topmost tower
To the eastward: up I climb'd a thousand steps
With pain: as in a dream I seem'd to climb
For ever: at the last I reach'd a door,
A light was in the crannies, and I heard,
'Glory and joy and honour to our Lord
And to the Holy Vessel of the Grail'.
Then in my madness I essay'd the door;
It gave; and thro' a stormy glare, a heat
As from a seventimes-heated furnace, I,
Blasted and burnt, and blinded as I was,
With such a fierceness that I swoon'd away—
O, yet methought I saw the Holy Grail,
All pall'd in crimson samite, and around
Great angels, awful shapes, and wings and eyes.

And but for all my madness and my sin,
And then my swooning, I had sworn I saw
That which I saw; but what I saw was veil'd
And cover'd; and this Quest was not for me.

* * *

PELLEAS AND ETTARRE

SONG BEFORE GUINEVERE

* * *

'A rose, but one, none other rose had I,
A rose, one rose, and this was wondrous fair,
One rose, a rose that gladden'd earth and sky,
One rose, my rose, that sweeten'd all mine air—
I cared not for the thorns; the thorns were there.

'One rose, a rose to gather by and by,
One rose, a rose, to gather and to wear,
No rose but one—what other rose had I?
One rose, my rose; a rose that will not die,—
He dies who loves it,—if the worm be there.'

* * *

THE RETURN OF SIR PELLEAS

But when he saw
High up in heaven the hall that Merlin built,
Blackening against the dead-green stripes of even,
'Black nest of rats', he groan'd, 'ye build too high'.

* * *

                              The Queen
Look'd hard upon her lover, he on her;
And each foresaw the dolorous day to be:
And all talk died, as in a grove all song
Beneath the shadow of some bird of prey;
Then a long silence came upon the hall,
And Modred thought, 'The time is hard at hand'.

THE LAST TOURNAMENT

KING ARTHUR AND THE RED KNIGHT

* * *

AND Arthur deign'd not use of word or sword,
   But let the drunkard, as he stretch'd from horse
   To strike him, overbalancing his bulk,
Down from the causeway heavily to the swamp
Fall, as the crest of some slow-arching wave,
Heard in dead night along that table-shore,
Drops flat, and after the great waters break
Whitening for half a league, and thin themselves,
Far over sands marbled with moon and cloud,
From less and less to nothing.

* * *

THE BURNING OF THE RED KNIGHT'S TOWER

Then, echoing yell with yell, they fired the tower,
Which half that autumn night, like the live North,
Red-pulsing up thro' Alioth and Alcor,
Made all above it, and a hundred meres

About it, as the water Moab saw
Come round by the East, and out beyond them flush'd
The long low dune, and lazy-plunging sea.

* * *

GUINEVERE

GUINEVERE'S FLIGHT

Queen Guinevere had fled the court, and sat
There in the holy house at Almesbury
Weeping, none with her save a little maid,
A novice: one low light betwixt them burn'd
Blurr'd by the creeping mist, for all abroad,
Beneath a moon unseen albeit at full,
The white mist, like a face-cloth to the face,
Clung to the dead earth, and the land was still.

* * *

MODRED REMEMBERS

But, ever after, the small violence done
Rankled in him and ruffled all his heart,
As the sharp wind that ruffles all day long
A little bitter pool about a stone
On the bare coast.

* * *

THE SIGNS AT ARTHUR'S COMING

To whom the little novice garrulously,
'Yea, but I know: the land was full of signs

And wonders ere the coming of the Queen.
So said my father, and himself was knight
Of the great Table—at the founding of it;
And rode thereto from Lyonnesse, and he said
That as he rode, an hour or maybe twain
After the sunset, down the coast, he heard
Strange music, and he paused, and turning—there,
All down the lonely coast of Lyonnesse,
Each with a beacon-star upon his head,
And with a wild sea-light about his feet,
He saw them—headland after headland flame
Far on into the rich heart of the west:
And in the light the white mermaiden swam,
And strong man-breasted things stood from the sea,
And sent a deep sea-voice thro' all the land,
To which the little elves of chasm and cleft
Made answer, sounding like a distant horn.
So said my father—yea, and furthermore,
Next morning, while he past the dim-lit woods,
Himself beheld three spirits mad with joy
Come dashing down on a tall wayside flower,
That shook beneath them, as the thistle shakes
When three gray linnets wrangle for the seed:
And still at evenings on before his horse
The flickering fairy-circle wheel'd and broke
Flying, and link'd again, and wheel'd and broke
Flying, for all the land was full of life.
And when at last he came to Camelot,
A wreath of airy dancers hand-in-hand
Swung round the lighted lantern of the hall;
And in the hall itself was such a feast
As never man had dream'd; for every knight

Had whatsoever meat he long'd for served
By hands unseen; and even as he said
Down in the cellars merry bloated things
Shoulder'd the spigot, straddling on the butts
While the wine ran: so glad were spirits and men
Before the coming of the sinful Queen'.

   Then spake the Queen and somewhat bitterly,
'Were they so glad? ill prophets were they all,
Spirits and men: could none of them foresee,
Not even thy wise father with his signs
And wonders, what has fall'n upon the realm?'

   To whom the novice garrulously again,
'Yea, one, a bard; of whom my father said,
Full many a noble war-song had he sung,
Ev'n in the presence of an enemy's fleet,
Between the steep cliff and the coming wave;
And many a mystic lay of life and death
Had chanted on the smoky mountain-tops,
When round him bent the spirits of the hills
With all their dewy hair blown back like flame:
So said my father—and that night the bard
Sang Arthur's glorious wars, and sang the King
As wellnigh more than man, and rail'd at those
Who call'd him the false son of Gorloïs:
For there was no man knew from whence he came;
But after tempest, when the long wave broke
All down the thundering shores of Bude and Bos,
There came a day as still as heaven, and then
They found a naked child upon the sands
Of dark Tintagil by the Cornish sea;
And that was Arthur; and they foster'd him

Till he by miracle was approven King:
And that his grave should be a mystery
From all men, like his birth; and could he find
A woman in her womanhood as great
As he was in his manhood, then, he sang,
The twain together well might change the world.
But even in the middle of his song
He falter'd, and his hand fell from the harp,
And pale he turn'd, and reel'd, and would have fall'n,
But that they stay'd him up; nor would he tell
His vision; but what doubt that he foresaw
This evil work of Lancelot and the Queen?'

*   *   *

THE PARTING OF ARTHUR AND GUINEVERE

And while he spake to these his helm was lower'd,
To which for crest the golden dragon clung
Of Britain; so she did not see the face,
Which then was as an angel's, but she saw,
Wet with the mists and smitten by the lights,
The Dragon of the great Pendragonship
Blaze, making all the night a steam of fire.
And even then he turn'd; and more and more
The moony vapour rolling round the King,
Who seem'd the phantom of a Giant in it,
Enwound him fold by fold, and made him gray
And grayer, till himself became as mist
Before her, moving ghostlike to his doom.

*   *   *

THE PASSING OF ARTHUR

THE END OF ARTHUR'S LAST BATTLE

* * *

Only the wan wave
Brake in among dead faces, to and fro
Swaying the helpless hands, and up and down
Tumbling the hollow helmets of the fallen,
And shiver'd brands that once had fought with Rome,
And rolling far along the gloomy shores
The voice of days of old and days to be.

* * *

THE REVENGE

A BALLAD OF THE FLEET

I

AT FLORES in the Azores Sir Richard Grenville lay,
   And a pinnace, like a flutter'd bird, came flying from
     far away:
'Spanish ships of war at sea! we have sighted fifty-three!'
Then sware Lord Thomas Howard: ''Fore God I am no coward;
But I cannot meet them here, for my ships are out of gear,
And the half my men are sick. I must fly, but follow quick.
We are six ships of the line; can we fight with fifty-three?'

II

Then spake Sir Richard Grenville: 'I know you are no coward;
You fly them for a moment to fight with them again.
But I've ninety men and more that are lying sick ashore.

I should count myself the coward if I left them, my Lord Howard,
To these Inquisition dogs and the devildoms of Spain'.

III

So Lord Howard past away with five ships of war that day,
Till he melted like a cloud in the silent summer heaven;
But Sir Richard bore in hand all his sick men from the land
Very carefully and slow,
Men of Bideford in Devon,
And we laid them on the ballast down below;
For we brought them all aboard,
And they blest him in their pain, that they were not left to Spain,
To the thumbscrew and the stake, for the glory of the Lord.

IV

He had only a hundred seamen to work the ship and to fight,
And he sailed away from Flores till the Spaniard came in sight,
With his huge sea-castles heaving upon the weather bow.
'Shall we fight or shall we fly?
Good Sir Richard, tell us now,
For to fight is but to die!
There'll be little of us left by the time this sun be set.'
And Sir Richard said again: 'We be all good English men.
Let us bang these dogs of Seville, the children of the devil,
For I never turn'd my back upon Don or devil yet'.

V

Sir Richard spoke and he laugh'd, and we roar'd a hurrah, and so
The little Revenge ran on sheer into the heart of the foe,
With her hundred fighters on deck, and her ninety sick below;

For half of their fleet to the right and half to the left were seen,
And the little Revenge ran on thro' the long sea-lane between.

VI

Thousands of their soldiers look'd down from their decks and laugh'd,
Thousands of their seamen made mock at the mad little craft Running on and on, till delay'd
By their mountain-like San Philip that, of fifteen hundred tons,
And up-shadowing high above us with her yawning tiers of guns,
Took the breath from our sails, and we stay'd.

VII

And while now the great San Philip hung above us like a cloud
Whence the thunderbolt will fall
Long and loud,
Four galleons drew away
From the Spanish fleet that day,
And two upon the larboard and two upon the starboard lay,
And the battle-thunder broke from them all.

VIII

But anon the great San Philip, she bethought herself and went
Having that within her womb that had left her ill content;
And the rest they came aboard us, and they fought us hand to hand,
For a dozen times they came with their pikes and musqueteers,
And a dozen times we shook 'em off as a dog that shakes his ears
When he leaps from the water to the land.

IX

And the sun went down, and the stars came out far over the summer sea,
But never a moment ceased the fight of the one and the fifty-three.
Ship after ship, the whole night long, their high-built galleons came,
Ship after ship, the whole night long, with her battle-thunder and flame;
Ship after ship, the whole night long, drew back with her dead and her shame.
For some were sunk and many were shatter'd, and so could fight us no more—
God of battles, was ever a battle like this in the world before?

X

For he said 'Fight on! fight on!'
Tho' his vessel was all but a wreck;
And it chanced that, when half of the short summer night was gone,
With a grisly wound to be drest he had left the deck,
But a bullet struck him that was dressing it suddenly dead,
And himself he was wounded again in the side and the head,
And he said 'Fight on! fight on!'

XI

And the night went down, and the sun smiled out far over the summer sea,
And the Spanish fleet with broken sides lay round us all in a ring;
But they dared not touch us again, for they fear'd that we still could sting,

So they watch'd what the end would be.
And we had not fought them in vain,
But in perilous plight were we,
Seeing forty of our poor hundred were slain,
And half of the rest of us maim'd for life
In the crash of the cannonades and the desperate strife;
And the sick men down in the hold were most of them stark and cold,
And the pikes were all broken or bent, and the powder was all of it spent;
And the masts and the rigging were lying over the side;
But Sir Richard cried in his English pride,
'We have fought such a fight for a day and a night
As may never be fought again!
We have won great glory, my men!
And a day less or more
At sea or ashore,
We die—does it matter when?
Sink me the ship, Master Gunner—sink her, split her in twain!
Fall into the hands of God, not into the hands of Spain!'

XII

And the gunner said 'Ay, ay', but the seamen made reply:
'We have children, we have wives,
And the Lord hath spared our lives.
We will make the Spaniard promise, if we yield, to let us go;
We shall live to fight again and to strike another blow'.
And the lion there lay dying, and they yielded to the foe.

XIII

And the stately Spanish men to their flagship bore him then,
Where they laid him by the mast, old Sir Richard caught at last,

And they praised him to his face with their courtly foreign grace;
But he rose upon their decks, and he cried:
'I have fought for Queen and Faith like a valiant man and true;
I have only done my duty as a man is bound to do:
With a joyful spirit I Sir Richard Grenville die!'
And he fell upon their decks, and he died.

XIV

And they stared at the dead that had been so valiant and true,
And had holden the power and glory of Spain so cheap
That he dared her with one little ship and his English few;
Was he devil or man? He was devil for aught they knew,
But they sank his body with honour down into the deep,
And they mann'd the Revenge with a swarthier alien crew,
And away she sail'd with her loss and long'd for her own;
When a wind from the lands they had ruin'd awoke from sleep,
And the water began to heave and the weather to moan,
And or ever that evening ended a great gale blew,
And a wave like the wave that is raised by an earthquake grew,
Till it smote on their hulls and their sails and their masts and their flags,
And the whole sea plunged and fell on the shot-shatter'd navy of Spain,
And the little Revenge herself went down by the island crags
To be lost evermore in the main.

THE VOYAGE OF MAELDUNE

(FOUNDED ON AN IRISH LEGEND. A.D. 700)

I.

I was the chief of the race—he had stricken my father dead—
But I gather'd my fellows together, I swore I would strike off his head.
Each of them look'd like a king, and was noble in birth as in worth,
And each of them boasted he sprang from the oldest race upon earth.
Each was as brave in the fight as the bravest hero of song,
And each of them liefer had died than have done one another a wrong.
He lived on an isle in the ocean—we sail'd on a Friday morn—
He that had slain my father the day before I was born.

II

And we came to the isle in the ocean, and there on the shore was he.
But a sudden blast blew us out and away thro' a boundless sea.

III

And we came to the Silent Isle that we never had touch'd at before,
Where a silent ocean always broke on a silent shore,
And the brooks glitter'd on in the light without sound, and the long waterfalls
Pour'd in a thunderless plunge to the base of the mountain walls,

And the poplar and cypress unshaken by storm flourish'd up beyond sight,
And the pine shot aloft from the crag to an unbelievable height,
And high in the heaven above it there flicker'd a songless lark,
And the cock couldn't crow, and the bull couldn't low, and the dog couldn't bark.
And round it we went, and thro' it, but never a murmur, a breath—
It was all of it fair as life, it was all of it quiet as death,
And we hated the beautiful Isle, for whenever we strove to speak
Our voices were thinner and fainter than any flittermouse-shriek;
And the men that were mighty of tongue and could raise such a battle-cry
That a hundred who heard it would rush on a thousand lances and die—
O they to be dumb'd by the charm!—so fluster'd with anger were they
They almost fell on each other; but after we sail'd away.

IV

And we came to the Isle of Shouting, we landed, a score of wild birds
Cried from the topmost summit with human voices and words;
Once in an hour they cried, and whenever their voices peal'd
The steer fell down at the plow and the harvest died from the field,
And the men dropt dead in the valleys and half of the cattle went lame,
And the roof sank in on the hearth, and the dwelling broke into flame;

And the shouting of these wild birds ran into the hearts of my crew,
Till they shouted along with the shouting and seized one another and slew;
But I drew them the one from the other; I saw that we could not stay,
And we left the dead to the birds and we sail'd with our wounded away.

V

And we came to the Isle of Flowers: their breath met us out on the seas,
For the Spring and the middle Summer sat each on the lap of the breeze;
And the red passion-flower to the cliffs, and the dark-blue clematis, clung,
And starr'd with a myriad blossom the long convolvulus hung;
And the topmost spire of the mountain was lilies in lieu of snow,
And the lilies like glaciers winded down, running out below
Thro' the fire of the tulip and poppy, the blaze of gorse, and the blush
Of millions of roses that sprang without leaf or a thorn from the bush;
And the whole isle-side flashing down from the peak without ever a tree
Swept like a torrent of gems from the sky to the blue of the sea;
And we roll'd upon capes of crocus and vaunted our kith and our kin,
And we wallow'd in beds of lilies, and chanted the triumph of Finn,

Till each like a golden image was pollen'd from head to feet
And each was as dry as a cricket, with thirst in the middle-day heat.
Blossom and blossom, and promise of blossom, but never a fruit!
And we hated the Flowering Isle, as we hated the isle that was mute,
And we tore up the flowers by the million and flung them in bight and bay,
And we left but a naked rock, and in anger we sail'd away.

VI

And we came to the Isle of Fruits: all round from the cliffs and the capes,
Purple or amber, dangled a hundred fathom of grapes,
And the warm melon lay like a little sun on the tawny sand,
And the fig ran up from the beach and rioted over the land,
And the mountain arose like a jewell'd throne thro' the fragrant air,
Glowing with all-colour'd plums and with golden masses of pear,
And the crimson and scarlet of berries that flamed upon bine and vine,
But in every berry and fruit was the poisonous pleasure of wine;
And the peak of the mountain was apples, the hugest that ever were seen,
And they prest, as they grew, on each other, with hardly a leaflet between,
And all of them redder than rosiest health or than utterest shame,
And setting, when Even descended, the very sunset aflame;

And we stay'd three days, and we gorged and we madden'd,
    till every one drew
His sword on his fellow to slay him, and ever they struck and
    they slew;
And myself, I had eaten but sparely, and fought till I sunder'd
    the fray,
Then I bad them remember my father's death, and we sail'd
    away.

VII

And we came to the Isle of Fire: we were lured by the light
    from afar,
For the peak sent up one league of fire to the Northern Star;
Lured by the glare and the blare, but scarcely could stand
    upright,
For the whole isle shudder'd and shook like a man in a mortal
    affright;
We were giddy besides with the fruits we had gorged, and so
    crazed that at last
There were some leap'd into the fire; and away we sail'd, and
    we past
Over that undersea isle, where the water is clearer than air:
Down we look'd: what a garden! O bliss, what a Paradise
    there!
Towers of a happier time, low down in a rainbow deep
Silent palaces, quiet fields of eternal sleep!
And three of the gentlest and best of my people, whate'er I
    could say,
Plunged head down in the sea, and the Paradise trembled
    away.

VIII

And we came to the Bounteous Isle, where the heavens lean
 low on the land,
And ever at dawn from the cloud glitter'd o'er us a sunbright
 hand,
Then it open'd and dropt at the side of each man, as he rose
 from his rest,
Bread enough for his need till the labourless day dipt under
 the West;
And we wander'd about it and thro' it. O never was time so
 good!
And we sang of the triumphs of Finn, and the boast of our
 ancient blood,
And we gazed at the wandering wave as we sat by the gurgle of
 springs,
And we chanted the songs of the Bards and the glories of fairy
 kings;
But at length we began to be weary, to sigh, and to stretch and
 yawn,
Till we hated the Bounteous Isle and the sunbright hand of the
 dawn,
For there was not an enemy near, but the whole green Isle was
 our own,
And we took to playing at ball, and we took to throwing the
 stone,
And we took to playing at battle, but that was a perilous play,
For the passion of battle was in us, we slew and we sail'd away.

IX

And we past to the Isle of Witches and heard their musical
 cry—
'Come to us, O come, come' in the stormy red of a sky

Dashing the fires and the shadows of dawn on the beautiful shapes,
For a wild witch naked as heaven stood on each of the loftiest capes,
And a hundred ranged on the rock like white sea-birds in a row,
And a hundred gamboll'd and pranced on the wrecks in the sand below,
And a hundred splash'd from the ledges, and bosom'd the burst of the spray,
But I knew we should fall on each other, and hastily sail'd away.

x

And we came in an evil time to the Isle of the Double Towers,
One was a smooth-cut stone, one carved all over with flowers,
But an earthquake always moved in the hollows under the dells,
And they shock'd on each other and butted each other with clashing of bells,
And the daws flew out of the Towers and jangled and wrangled in vain,
And the clash and boom of the bells rang into the heart and the brain,
Till the passion of battle was on us, and all took sides with the Towers,
There were some for the clean-cut stone, there were more for the carven flowers,
And the wrathful thunder of God peal'd over us all the day,
For the one half slew the other, and after we sail'd away.

XI

And we came to the Isle of a Saint who had sail'd with St Brendan of yore,
He had lived ever since on the Isle and his winters were fifteen score,
And his voice was low as from other worlds, and his eyes were sweet,
And his white hair sank to his heels and his white beard fell to his feet,
And he spake to me, 'O Maeldune, let be this purpose of thine!
Remember the words of the Lord when he told us "Vengeance is mine!"
His fathers have slain thy fathers in war or in single strife,
Thy fathers have slain his fathers, each taken a life for a life,
Thy father had slain his father, how long shall the murder last?
Go back to the Isle of Finn and suffer the Past to be Past'.
And we kiss'd the fringe of his beard and we pray'd as we heard him pray,
And the Holy man he assoil'd us, and sadly we sail'd away.

XII

And we came to the Isle we were blown from, and there on the shore was he,
The man that had slain my father. I saw him and let him be.
O weary was I of the travel, the trouble, the strife and the sin,
When I landed again, with a tithe of my men, on the Isle of Finn.

TIRESIAS

* * *

　　　　　　　　　　But for me,
I would that I were gather'd to my rest,
And mingled with the famous kings of old,
On whom about their ocean-islets flash
The faces of the Gods—the wise man's word,
Here trampled by the populace underfoot,
There crown'd with worship—and these eyes will find
The men I knew, and watch the chariot whirl
About the goal again, and hunters race
The shadowy lion, and the warrior-kings,
In height and prowess more than human, strive
Again for glory, while the golden lyre
Is ever sounding in heroic ears
Heroic hymns, and every way the vales
Wind, clouded with the grateful incense-fume
Of those who mix all odour to the Gods
On one far height in one far-shining fire.

* * *

LOCKSLEY HALL SIXTY YEARS AFTER

* * *

Gone the fires of youth, the follies, furies, curses, passionate tears,
Gone like fires and floods and earthquakes of the planet's dawning years.

Fires that shook me once, but now to silent ashes fall'n away.
Cold upon the dead volcano sleeps the gleam of dying day.

Gone the tyrant of my youth, and mute below the chancel stones,
All his virtues—I forgive them—black in white above his bones.

* * *

TO VIRGIL

WRITTEN AT THE REQUEST OF THE MANTUANS FOR THE NINETEENTH CENTENARY OF VIRGIL'S DEATH

I

ROMAN VIRGIL, thou that singest
    Ilion's lofty temples robed in fire,
    Ilion falling, Rome arising,
wars, and filial faith, and Dido's pyre;

II

Landscape-lover, lord of language
    more than he that sang the Works and Days,
All the chosen coin of fancy
    flashing out from many a golden phrase;

III

Thou that singest wheat and woodland,
    tilth and vineyard, hive and horse and herd;
All the charm of all the Muses
    often flowering in a lonely word;

IV

Poet of the happy Tityrus
    piping underneath his beechen bowers;
Poet of the poet-satyr
    whom the laughing shepherd bound with flowers;

V

Chanter of the Pollio, glorying
    in the blissful years again to be,
Summers of the snakeless meadow,
    unlaborious earth and oarless sea;

VI

Thou that seëst Universal
    Nature moved by Universal Mind;
Thou majestic in thy sadness
    at the doubtful doom of human kind;

VII

Light among the vanish'd ages;
    star that gildest yet this phantom shore;
Golden branch amid the shadows,
    kings and realms that pass to rise no more;

VIII

Now thy Forum roars no longer,
    fallen every purple Cæsar's dome—
Tho' thine ocean-roll of rhythm
    sound for ever of Imperial Rome—

IX

Now the Rome of slaves hath perish'd,
    and the Rome of freemen holds her place,
I, from out the Northern Island
    sunder'd once from all the human race,

X

I salute thee, Mantovano,
    I that loved thee since my day began,
Wielder of the stateliest measure
    ever moulded by the lips of man.

'FRATER AVE ATQUE VALE'

Row us out from Desenzano, to your Sirmione row!
 So they row'd, and there we landed—'O venusta Sirmio!'
There to me thro' all the groves of olive in the summer glow,
There beneath the Roman ruin where the purple flowers grow,
Came that 'Ave atque Vale' of the Poet's hopeless woe,
Tenderest of Roman poets nineteen-hundred years ago,
'Frater Ave atque Vale'—as we wander'd to and fro
Gazing at the Lydian laughter of the Garda Lake below
Sweet Catullus's all-but-island, olive-silvery Sirmio!

THE PROGRESS OF SPRING

I

The groundflame of the crocus breaks the mould,
 Fair Spring slides hither o'er the Southern sea,
 Wavers on her thin stem the snowdrop cold
That trembles not to kisses of the bee:
Come, Spring, for now from all the dripping eaves
 The spear of ice has wept itself away,
And hour by hour unfolding woodbine leaves
 O'er his uncertain shadow droops the day.
She comes! The loosen'd rivulets run;
 The frost-bead melts upon her golden hair;
Her mantle, slowly greening in the Sun,
 Now wraps her close, now arching leaves her bare
 To breaths of balmier air;

II

Up leaps the lark, gone wild to welcome her,
    About her glance the tits, and shriek the jays,
Before her skims the jubilant woodpecker,
    The linnet's bosom blushes at her gaze,
While round her brows a woodland culver flits,
    Watching her large light eyes and gracious looks,
And in her open palm a halcyon sits
    Patient—the secret splendour of the brooks.
Come, Spring! She comes on waste and wood,
    On farm and field: but enter also here,
Diffuse thyself at will thro' all my blood,
    And, tho' thy violet sicken into sere,
    Lodge with me all the year!

III

Once more a downy drift against the brakes,
    Self-darken'd in the sky, descending slow!
But gladly see I thro' the wavering flakes
    Yon blanching apricot like snow in snow.
These will thine eyes not brook in forest-paths,
    On their perpetual pine, nor round the beech;
They fuse themselves to little spicy baths,
    Solved in the tender blushes of the peach;
They lose themselves and die
    On that new life that gems the hawthorn line;
Thy gay lent-lilies wave and put them by,
    And out once more in varnish'd glory shine
    Thy stars of celandine.

IV

She floats across the hamlet. Heaven lours,
   But in the tearful splendour of her smiles
I see the slowly-thickening chestnut towers
   Fill out the spaces by the barren tiles.
Now past her feet the swallow circling flies,
   A clamorous cuckoo stoops to meet her hand;
Her light makes rainbows in my closing eyes,
   I hear a charm of song thro' all the land.
Come, Spring! She comes, and Earth is glad
   To roll her North below thy deepening dome,
But ere thy maiden birk be wholly clad,
   And these low bushes dip their twigs in foam,
   Make all true hearths thy home.

V

Across my garden! and the thicket stirs,
   The fountain pulses high in sunnier jets,
The blackcap warbles, and the turtle purrs,
   The starling claps his tiny castanets.
Still round her forehead wheels the woodland dove,
   And scatters on her throat the sparks of dew,
The kingcup fills her footprint, and above
   Broaden the glowing isles of vernal blue.
Hail ample presence of a Queen,
   Bountiful, beautiful, apparell'd gay,
Whose mantle, every shade of glancing green,
   Flies back in fragrant breezes to display
   A tunic white as May!

VI

She whispers, 'From the South I bring you balm,
    For on a tropic mountain was I born,
While some dark dweller by the coco-palm
    Watch'd my far meadow zoned with airy morn;
From under rose a muffled moan of floods;
    I sat beneath a solitude of snow;
There no one came, the turf was fresh, the woods
    Plunged gulf on gulf thro' all their vales below.
I saw beyond their silent tops
    The steaming marshes of the scarlet cranes,
The slant seas leaning on the mangrove copse,
    And summer basking in the sultry plains
    About a land of canes;

VII

'Then from my vapour-girdle soaring forth
    I scaled the buoyant highway of the birds,
And drank the dews and drizzle of the North,
    That I might mix with men, and hear their words
On pathway'd plains; for—while my hand exults
    Within the bloodless heart of lowly flowers
To work old laws of Love to fresh results,
    Thro' manifold effect of simple powers—
I too would teach the man
    Beyond the darker hour to see the bright,
That his fresh life may close as it began,
    The still-fulfilling promise of a light
    Narrowing the bounds of night'.

VIII

So wed thee with my soul, that I may mark
    The coming year's great good and varied ills,
And new developments, whatever spark
    Be struck from out the clash of warring wills;
Or whether, since our nature cannot rest,
    The smoke of war's volcano burst again
From hoary deeps that belt the changeful West,
    Old Empires, dwellings of the kings of men;
Or should those fail, that hold the helm,
    While the long day of knowledge grows and warms,
And in the heart of this most ancient realm
    A hateful voice be utter'd, and alarms
    Sounding 'To arms! to arms!'

IX

A simpler, saner lesson might he learn
    Who reads thy gradual process, Holy Spring.
Thy leaves possess the season in their turn,
    And in their time thy warblers rise on wing.
How surely glidest thou from March to May,
    And changest, breathing it, the sullen wind,
Thy scope of operation, day by day,
    Larger and fuller, like the human mind!
Thy warmths from bud to bud
    Accomplish that blind model in the seed,
And men have hopes, which race the restless blood,
    That after many changes may succeed
    Life which is Life indeed.

MERLIN AND THE GLEAM

I

O YOUNG Mariner,
You from the haven
Under the sea-cliff,
You that are watching
The gray Magician
With eyes of wonder,
I am Merlin,
And *I* am dying,
I am Merlin
Who follow The Gleam.

II

Mighty the Wizard
Who found me at sunrise
Sleeping, and woke me
And learn'd me Magic!
Great the Master,
And sweet the Magic,
When over the valley,
In early summers,
Over the mountain,
On human faces,
And all around me,
Moving to melody,
Floated The Gleam.

III

Once at the croak of a Raven who crost it,
A barbarous people,
Blind to the magic,

And deaf to the melody,
Snarl'd at and cursed me.
A demon vext me,
The light retreated,
The landskip darken'd,
The melody deaden'd,
The Master whisper'd
'Follow the Gleam'.

IV

Then to the melody,
Over a wilderness
Gliding, and glancing at
Elf of the woodland,
Gnome of the cavern,
Griffin and Giant,
And dancing of Fairies
In desolate hollows,
And wraiths of the mountain,
And rolling of dragons
By warble of water,
Or cataract music
Of falling torrents,
Flitted The Gleam.

V

Down from the mountain
And over the level,
And streaming and shining on
Silent river,
Silvery willow,
Pasture and plowland,

Innocent maidens,
Garrulous children,
Homestead and harvest,
Reaper and gleaner,
And rough-ruddy faces
Of lowly labour,
Slided The Gleam—

VI

Then, with a melody
Stronger and statelier,
Led me at length
To the city and palace
Of Arthur the king;
Touch'd at the golden
Cross of the churches,
Flash'd on the Tournament
Flicker'd and bicker'd
From helmet to helmet,
And last on the forehead
Of Arthur the blameless
Rested The Gleam.

VII

Clouds and darkness
Closed upon Camelot;
Arthur had vanish'd
I knew not whither,
The king who loved me,
And cannot die;
For out of the darkness
Silent and slowly

The Gleam, that had waned to a wintry
    glimmer
On icy fallow
And faded forest,
Drew to the valley
Named of the shadow,
And slowly brightening
Out of the glimmer,
And slowly moving again to a melody
Yearningly tender,
Fell on the shadow,
No longer a shadow,
But clothed with The Gleam.

VIII

And broader and brighter
The Gleam flying onward,
Wed to the melody,
Sang thro' the world;
And slower and fainter,
Old and weary,
But eager to follow,
I saw, whenever
In passing it glanced upon
Hamlet or city,
That under the Crosses
The dead man's garden,
The mortal hillock,
Would break into blossom;
And so to the land's
Last limit I came—
And can no longer,

But die rejoicing,
For thro' the Magic
Of Him the Mighty,
Who taught me in childhood,
There on the border
Of boundless Ocean,
And all but in Heaven
Hovers The Gleam.

IX

Not of the sunlight,
Not of the moonlight,
Not of the starlight!
O young Mariner,
Down to the haven,
Call your companions,
Launch your vessel,
And crowd your canvas,
And, ere it vanishes
Over the margin,
After it, follow it,
Follow The Gleam.

JUNE BRACKEN AND HEATHER

TO E. T.

THERE on the top of the down,
    The wild heather round me and over me June's high blue,
When I look'd at the bracken so bright and the heather so brown,

I thought to myself I would offer this book to you,
This, and my love together,
To you that are seventy-seven,
With a faith as clear as the heights of the June-blue heaven,
And a fancy as summer-new
As the green of the bracken amid the gloom of the heather.

ST TELEMACHUS

* * *

    And once, he thought, a shape with wings
Came sweeping by him, and pointed to the West,
And at his ear he heard a whisper 'Rome'
And in his heart he cried 'The call of God!'
And call'd arose, and, slowly plunging down
Thro' that disastrous glory, set his face
By waste and field and town of alien tongue,
Following a hundred sunsets, and the sphere
Of westward-wheeling stars; and every dawn
Struck from him his own shadow on to Rome.

* * *

CROSSING THE BAR

SUNSET and evening star,
   And one clear call for me!
And may there be no moaning of the bar,
   When I put out to sea,

But such a tide as moving seems asleep,
    Too full for sound and foam,
When that which drew from out the boundless deep
    Turns again home.

Twilight and evening bell,
    And after that the dark!
And may there be no sadness of farewell,
    When I embark;

For tho' from out our bourne of Time and Place
    The flood may bear me far,
I hope to see my Pilot face to face
    When I have crost the bar.

821.8 Tennyson
Tennyson, Alfred Tennyson,
Alfred, Lord Tennyson
30519010406539

PROPERTY OF
HIGH POINT PUBLIC LIBRARY
HIGH POINT, NORTH CAROLINA

CPSIA information can be obtained
at www.ICGtesting.com
Printed in the USA
BVHW031321161118
533306BV00001B/21/P